Coyote Says . . .
More Conversations With God's Dog

by Webster Kitchell

Skinner House Books
Boston

Published by Skinner House Books, an imprint of the Unitarian Universalist Association, 25 Beacon Street, Boston, MA 02108-2800.

ISBN 1-55896-345-6

Printed in Canada.

"Coyote and the Mutant Message Down Under" was previously published in the Unitarian Universalist Psi Symposium Annual Journal, Fall 1995 issue.

10 9 8 7 6 5 4 3 2
05 04 03 02 01 00

CONTENTS

THE WHY OF COYOTE

At a Unitarian Universalist General Assembly, I was asked about Anglos taking over Native American mythic figures. I also have been told that Anglos have a naive and sentimental view of Native Americans.

Both of these views are good criticisms. My response is that Coyote and I are not playing "feel good" games here. We are doing some hard work rethinking the mythic foundations of our culture. I know a lot of Unitarian Universalists think myth is something we have outgrown, that we should look to technology and rationality as guides out of our predicament. I happen to believe that's a myth. It may be a good and useful myth, but when we don't recognize a myth for what it is, we are in danger of being fundamentalists, spending our energy defensively protecting the literal truth of our myth and ignoring the consequences of our collective, human, willful ignorance of what is real.

I find Coyote, the Trickster, an incarnation of all in me that is not rational, that still screams to be alive in a technically suffocating culture. I find Coyote to be a magical animal, an incarnation of what I experience in myself as earthy spirituality.

A revolution is going on against the technological, rational, and corporate sentiments that dominate our culture. It is a revolution saying "No!" at a primal, spiritual, life-and-death, wounded animal level. The proof of the deadliness of our rational, technical, corporate culture is the depression that greets us when we open the morning paper or listen to the evening news. We feel that it's all too late, that greed and denial are at the controls. Well, we're all going to die anyway, so we might as well have fun whacking a few myths as we go. It's a different path we're trying to discover again. We think it's a path to being whole, finding our animal nature. So I talk to my animal nature and it responds with a healing intelligence. I invite you to discuss things with your own animal nature and see if you find a wise voice you have overlooked.

COYOTE WANTS TO KNOW WHAT
THE GREAT ARCHITECT HAD IN MIND

 had been on vacation while Coyote went to a professional conference with Raven and some other tricksters in the lower levels of the pantheon. Once I was home and recovered, I left a G-mail message for him on universe-wide web. "G-mail," in case you didn't know, is restricted to requests of the gods and has replaced prayer in up-to-date religions. We arranged a mutual materialization at the donut shop. I arrived in my modish four-wheel drive vehicle, and he materialized in a way that still mystifies me. My spiritual goal is to acquire enough beneficence points to get a free out-of-body travel experience.

"So," I said, "how was the Tricksters' Conference?"

"Depressing," he said. "The House of Representatives in Washington and the Governor of New Mexico are stealing all our best material. It's a depressing time for minor local deities. Humans don't believe there is justice in the universe, therefore, they have no reason to avoid the morally outrageous. What's that you ordered?"

"An oat-bran donut," I said. "It's surprisingly good."

"I think I'll be sensible and have one, too."

"Coyote, please! You're a deity! You can do whatever you want with no consequences! We who are bound by life and death and space and time need you to look up to and envy! You gods can get away with what we can't."

"You don't need gods anymore," he said. He seemed somber. "You have your own egos to worship. You don't need us."

"Coyote, *compadre*, we *do*! We need something greater than ourselves to look up to."

"That's what I mean. You have your egos. Your egos are greater than you. You worship them. In the words of your own tradition, they lead you into temptation and damnation for their name's sake. Your egos lead you beside the dead waters. You preparest a table for your egos in the midst of starving humans and destroyed species. Yea, though you walk through the valley of the shadow of death, you foolishly fear no evil. But reality's rod and reality's staff will destroy you, and you will all die in a fool's paradise."

"Coyote! Don't say things like that! What were they serving at that pantheon conference?"

"Oh, it was rich!" he said. "We finally voted to call in the Architect of Creation and take Her to task. We were all set to vote a censure resolution and evict Her from the pantheon. I mean the gods were upset! Even the sub-working group of tricksters, all of whom are master cynics, felt the tricks of the humans had gone too far. A little respect for boundaries, please! A little respect for order, please!"

"What was the response of the Divine Architect to this move for censure?"

"She blamed the liberals."

"She what?"

"She blamed the liberals!"

"The liberal gods?"

"The liberal humans!"

I was stunned. I knew a church that wasn't going to take this revelation with equanimity. It was bad enough to lose the House of Representatives and the Senate, but we had always assumed we were still in favor with the gods!

"How could the Divine Architect say the liberals are to blame for the state of the planet?" I asked, horrified and not wanting to know the truth.

"Well," he said in a conspiratorial whisper, "I think She was scapegoating. I think She really didn't have an answer to what went wrong with the divine plan, so She chose the liberals as an easy target. Straw souls, leading the lower classes into immorality and a lack of standards. You know."

"But we liberals are such good people," I exclaimed. "We have such sensitive values. We mean well. Our hearts are pure. We are *reasonable!*"

He looked stern and said, "You also don't believe in the gods. Bad politics! You say the human psyche has no limits to what it can become. The ancient Greeks called that 'hubris,' and it always led to tragedy. Sure, you're right that the gods don't literally exist. Even the gods know that. But the limits the gods stand for have to be respected."

"I don't understand," I said, still in shock.

"Think a minute," he said. "Think about some of the gods you humans have created. You created Eros, love, yet the essence of love is to let be. You want to control. You created Dionysius, pleasure in the goodness of the earth and nature, yet you developed and paved nature. You created Jehovah, the god of justice for the victims of human greed. Now you sell justice to the rich. You created Jesus, the god of compassion in the face of human righteousness. Now you pillory the confused and the young and the neglected, the waifs and the unwed mothers and the unfathered fathers with a mean-spirited morality of the bottom-line."

My god, I thought, he's transformed himself from a coyote into an Old Testament prophet!

"I caught that thought," he said. "You're right, this is nothing new. But in Old Testament times humans had a sense of limits, and when the limits were transgressed, a prophet arose to call the culture to justice and decency. You don't have any prophets because you have no sense of limits imposed by time, space, life, or death. You think there is no certainty, all things are relative. One opinion is as good as the next, and all anyone has is opinion. No conviction."

"And you think liberals are to blame?" I asked, even more incredulous.

"I said you were scapegoats," he said, "but you set yourselves up."

"How?" I asked.

"By being reasonable," he said.

"By being reasonable?" I asked, even more incredulous.

"I wish you wouldn't keep repeating what I say," he said. "You are reasonable, right?"

"Of course," I said, "Unitarian Universalists are always reasonable!"

"And do they ever agree on what the problem is or what to do about it?"

"Of course not," I said. "It isn't reasonable to expect a reasonable group to agree on anything. There are too many different reasonable arguments and positions to agree."

"And yet you decry what is happening to the planet?" he asked.

"We feel as though we are a voice crying in the wilderness."

"And what does this voice crying in the wilderness proclaim?" he asked.

"We'll think about it." I said.

"You mean you'll think about what you're going to proclaim?" he asked, puzzled.

"No," I said. "What we proclaim in the wilderness is that we're going to think about it."

He was silent. He signalled for some more bran donuts and coffee. He ate a donut. He drank some coffee. I got more and more uncomfortable. Another bran donut seemed reasonable in the situation, so I had one. Then he muttered half to himself,

"Maybe the Divine Architect wasn't far off."

He sighed. Then he said, "I read an article while teleporting back home after the conference. It said the dominating culture of our planet, the culture that is truly becoming planetwide and shaping all the decisions of humans, is corporate culture. This corporate culture is the culture of the rational. Governments, peasants, the middle class, the animals who are being disposed of, the fish in the sea, the birds of the air, the gods of the human imagination—all are being judged by the rational standards of corporate life."

"Which are?" I asked.

"Well, I'll tell you," he said in a frank and cynical tone. "They ain't the standards of Jesus or Jehovah or Eros or Dionysius or the Buddha. These personifications of what humans imagined they could be are utterly absent from the rational, planet-engulfing values of the trans-personal corporate culture."

"Which blesses those who believe in it," I said.

"Sometimes yes, sometimes no," he said. "Never trust a god to deliver on what you think your god promised. A god sees a sucker who believes, it brings out the trickster."

"Like downsizing the workforce or lobbying Congress to relieve them of the expense of environmental regulations or the injustice of fair-hiring practices?" I asked.

"Oh, you cynic!" he said. "They are doing that for the good of their customers, bringing them a better life."

"So," I said, "if I understand your drift, you're telling me the values that make humans humane—compassion, poetry, justice, love—are not the motives of the dominating modern human culture. In fact, the dominant culture of money and reason doesn't even pay lip service to these values anymore."

"I heard it said in your church that nobody cares anymore," he said. "Is that true?"

"No," I said, "it isn't true that no one cares. It's just that the levers of power to change things are not available to us. The levers of power are in the hands of the beneficiaries of power, the rich and the elite and their well-paid servants. The levers of power are not in the hands of the populists."

We meditated silently.

"What is the way to freedom, Coyote?" I asked.

"Stop rewarding the powerful."

"And how do we do *that*?" I asked.

"The same way you stopped rewarding the gods," he said, "by not believing in them."

"What good will that do?" I asked.

"Because they want their egos worshipped. They are narcissists. They need their egos fed. Their egos feed on the millions who worship them on TV. Even if they are hated, they are noticed and feared. Being narcissists, they have no concern for what they are doing to the planet or other people or other species. They worship themselves and require everyone else to worship them, too. They suck up worship."

"Is there any hope?" I asked, toying with the remains of a donut I had lost interest in.

"Of course," he said. "As long as there are gods like Buddha, Jesus, Eros, Dionysius, Jehovah, and me, who keep reminding you of the joy, pain, tragedy, and ecstasy of being alive, of being merely human in all its width and depth and height, you will understand that being a purely reasonable human is a death trip. More and more of you will choose life with its pain and limits and love and pleasures. Irrationality will save you!"

I tossed off the last dregs of my coffee, wiped my moustache on my shirt sleeve, clapped him on the shoulder, and said, "My little church is not going to like it, Coyote. They're not going to like it! They wait for a fair-minded messiah with a reasonable solution."

He grinned as we got down from the counter stools.

"Well," he said, showing all his teeth and exhaling a greasy breath, "that's why they've got us!"

"Let's go run over a suit!" I said.

"Nah," he said, "we have to be compassionate."

So we went skateboarding on the plaza instead.

COYOTE AND THE MUTANT MESSAGE DOWN UNDER

 went to the donut shop looking for Coyote. As I ordered my whole-wheat muffin, faithful that the universe would provide what I needed (though never at the moment I needed it), Coyote materialized beside me and said to the waitress, "The usual."

Which, as you know, is two dozen assorted, sugar-coated, jelly-filled donuts.

I paid and said, "Bring them with you!" and headed for the door.

He had his mouth open for the first willing donut to sacrifice itself to his need, and my preemptory order caught him by surprise. However, Coyote is always game for synchronicity, so off we went with a large box of donuts, one whole-wheat muffin, and two large black coffees.

"Where we going, Reverend?" he asked laconically.

"You'll see," I said. Soon we were heading down a sandy trail in four-wheel drive.

"Hey," he said, "I live out here! You could have saved me the trouble of coming into town."

"Well," I said confidently, "it was only a matter of you teleporting and materializing at my mental suggestion. It wasn't as if I had in-convenienced you!"

"What the hell!" he said, indignant. "You think my teleporting myself and materializing whenever you have an urgent spiritual need is a soft life? You humans are so demanding of your gods! You don't understand the energy field necessary to transport a poor starving coyote from Buckman Wells to the donut shop just like that—Shazam! If I'd known we were coming way out here, I'd have ordered an-other two dozen."

"Here," I said, "have mine!"

"That's a whole-wheat muffin! You can't teleport and materialize on health food! Health food is good for dematerializing, but it won't put you back together again on the other side. Much research has gone into this by coyotes and spiritually adept beings. Health food has been proven a one-way street to dematerialization."

I stopped by the Rio Grande, got out, and said, "Let's sit in the shade of that tree and listen to the river and watch the hawks and see what happens spiritually."

He got that look of concern a friend gets when you start acting weird. "Sure," he said in a calming tone of voice. "Sure, whatever you like, Reverend."

I settled down at the base of a scrubby tree, broke out my whole-wheat muffin and coffee, while he ate his donuts reflectively, which is at a rate of two bites per donut instead of one. We finished, brushed the crumbs off our fur, and I said, "I've got a problem, Coyote."

"Tell your local compassionate deity," he said soothingly.

"It's a marketing problem."

"A what?" He hadn't been expecting this.

"A spiritual marketing problem," I clarified. "I think liberalism is in trouble and humanism is out of style. I'm thinking of taking up New Age spirituality. That's where the religious market is."

"Jesus!" he said softly.

"No, not Jesus," I said. "Dematerializing. Getting off the planet and out of sin and evil and stuff like that."

"Away from moral relativity and the Uncertainty Principle?" he asked.

"Yeah, those, too."

"You think you should be selling certainty?"

"No, not certainty. I wouldn't go that far. Just a host of unexamined propositions that tend to make people feel better."

He grinned. "The sort that if they work demonstrate what you want demonstrated and if they don't work, demonstrate that you didn't have enough faith?"

"Ah, you understand!" I said.

"You're sure you're not doing that already?" he said with just a touch of sarcasm.

"Well, I've had your help doing it if I have," I responded with equal acidity.

"Come, come," he said. "We know there's a difference between play, which is religious and gives life meaning, and reason, which is boring."

"Nicely put," I said, feeling better. "I couldn't have said it better."

We glowed for each other. I was half afraid I was going to see his aura.

"I've been reading a bad book that is very popular," I said.

"I know the one you mean," he said. "That one about a middle-aged American woman who gets hijacked by some Australian aborigines and marched across the burning sands for two months barefoot, surviving on ants and kangaroos, and learns deep spiritual truths from primitive people who communicate telepathically. That one?"

"That's it," I said. "*Mutant Message Down Under.*"

"You don't seem to find it believable," he said calmly.

"It's a novel. It's not supposed to be believed. It's the religious message it tells that disturbs me."

"What bothers you?" he asked in his best professional counseling manner.

"Two things principally, other than that I think it's bad writing, which is not a theological vice. I see two theological vices in the book. First, that evil and pain are due to human misunderstanding of the way the world works. There is just enough truth in that idea that it's appealing. Certainly a misunderstanding of the way the world works does result in people expecting things they shouldn't expect. Or not expecting things they should have been smart enough to prepare for."

"Such as what?" he asked.

"Such as thinking that being good is a defense against pain and evil happening."

"Yes," he said. "On various occasions we have demonstrated to the satisfaction of us both that being good is its own punishment. You miss out on a lot of fun by being good. You should be in your office in front of a boring word processor, and I should be running down small animals to take home for the kids' dinner. But here we are enjoying ourselves sitting by a river discussing the meaning of life."

"Sin is grand, isn't it, Coyote?" My mood was improving by feeling irresponsible and not feeling guilty about it.

"What did our friend the middle-aged American lady learn in the burning desolation of her walkabout?" he asked.

"She learned that things are not important, that loving kindness and group solidarity pay off. She learned you can bear a lot more than you think you can if you think it's going to kill you. She was taught civilization is a distraction from spiritual fulfillment. She did learn some truths that are not new, but have probably been discussed by people since technology got started with the Neanderthals."

"Actually, it started before then," he said. "It was hotly debated among the gods whether letting evolution take its course with humans was a good idea or the end of the earthly paradise for the creatures already here. The conservatives among us lost. You can see we were right."

"So you think what *Mutant Message Down Under* has to say is true? So-called primitive humans have a higher spiritual nature?"

"It all depends on your point of view," he said. "If you think Internet has spiritual value, you won't get excited by primitive telepathic communication. If you like electronic entertainment and microwaved food, you won't appreciate the stark beauty of the desert or the sweetness of eating ants."

I added, "It's a lot easier to accept a primitive lifestyle in a novel where all the people's needs are met by a joyously cooperative universe."

"How does the universe cooperate in the story?"

I sighed. "The people are hungry and a herd of antelope appears. The oldest antelope accepts that its role is to give its life as a gift to these human beings. It willingly allows itself to be killed."

"I don't believe you," he said, shocked. "People are not that naive."

"When people want to believe, they believe. After all, who can contradict them? We can't ask the dead antelope whether it achieved a state of ecstasy as it gave its life for some wandering humans."

"You're a skeptic," he said sternly.

"Guilty as charged," I said, "which makes me wonder whether repackaging our message to merchandise it to New Age devotees will work. I have a lot of investment in my skepticism. I'm not sure I want to give it up. In fact, humanity has a lot invested in its skepticism. It has been a wonderful tool in clearing away a lot of foolish human misunderstanding and deliberate obfuscating disinformation by monarchs and princes of the church, not to mention certain contemporary television political evangelists."

"But doesn't your skepticism inhibit your accepting some spiritual truths?"

"I would rather have my skepticism than accept a truth that has no authority other than that a number of people wish it were true."

"Give me an example," he said.

"The example of evil and pain in human experience," I said. "Some say it doesn't exist. It only seems to exist. That idea makes me angry. Evil and pain do exist in human living. I suspect that people want to think evil and pain don't really exist for two motives. First, they hope they can escape it by denial, magic, or being good. Second, they don't want to be encumbered with compassion."

"You're a skeptic and a cynic," he said.

"Thank you," I said.

We beamed at each other. After all, we had established that we were sinners, skeptics, and cynics having a lovely time sitting by a rolling river with full stomachs and no way of anyone getting in touch with us to remind us of our shoulds and oughts.

We both said in unison, "Thank God for the lack of telepathic communication!"

"You had a second complaint against Marlo Morgan's book," he said. "What is that?"

"Same one I had about *The Celestine Prophecy*," I said. "The pure in heart are planning to leave the earth."

"I liked that in *The Celestine Prophecy*," he said. "You have to remember I was one of the conservatives who thought we shouldn't have allowed the genetic engineering that led to humans. I would encourage humans to leave the planet."

I ignored him. I had to operate as a human. "I think it's immoral for people who have realized a certain spiritual maturity, who think they see clearly, to cop out on their fellow humans by disappearing into the ozone. I assume that one of the major characteristics of a fully realized human in the spiritual sense is compassion."

"Like Mother Teresa?" he asked.

"Sure," I said, "why not? People honor her, but they don't emulate her. People run away from home to India so they can revel in Mother Teresa's aura. What we need is a little compassion right here in River City. Practical help for pain and suffering and standing up against evil, even trying to understand the evil that resides in what we often think of as good."

"How can good contain evil in it?" he asked.

"A stable economy is a good thing. But balancing the budget on the backs of the poor and the old and children's future is a good thing that has an evil element in it. It isn't helped by having all the well-meaning intelligent people float off the planet."

"Is there any balm in Gilead for those who choose to stay?" he asked.

"Sure there is," I said. "As far as we know, and we have to be humble about what we know, the only glimmer of a balm in Gilead is the idea that God lives in the creature—human, Coyote, or jack-rabbit—that understands compassion and lives, as well as she or he can, a life of compassion—intelligent compassion, tough-minded compassion, organized compassion, well-funded compassion."

Coyote took up the thought. "That little placard on your study wall that says God lives in the person who lives in love and the person (or creature) that lives in love lives in God."

I nodded to him smilingly. "That's it," I said. "Terrifyingly simple and difficult to do because we are all so innately selfish."

"And rightly selfish," he said. "Selfish leads to survival in a world that contains evil and pain, viewed from a personal perspective."

I said, "But for the spiritually mature, it's a selfishness that is augmented by compassion 'feeling with' another and knowing that others 'feel with' you."

"And I suppose," he said with a sly grin, "that you think this involves staying around on earth like a Boddhisatva and helping out, not wafting into Nirvana."

"Exactly," I said. "Right here on earth! Living compassionately and joyously in the here and now."

Coyote looked around at the river and the trees, the cliffs and the clouds. He sighed and said, "So, what do you make of it?"

"What do you mean, what do I make of it?"

"Come on," he said. "You reject the New Age merchandising.

You're a cynic and a sceptic about undemonstrated spirituality. You think plain-Jane humanist liberalism is inadequate and out of style. What do you have to tell the folks when you get back to town?"

I watched a cloud. "Couldn't I just stay out here and watch clouds? Do I have to go back?"

"You have to," he said. "You're not ready to be a coyote."

"Okay," I said. "Here goes! I think there is a flow in the Universe that people mistake for God's action. It isn't God's action, it's just the flow. Reality is flow. It's big stuff like planets and suns. It's human scale stuff like birth and getting older and dying. It's those cliffs and the river and the hawks and you and me. But it isn't God working. It's the flow, mostly time and gravity and chemistry."

"Okay," he said, "so God's not in the flow. Where is God in this?"

"I thought maybe God was in the creative intelligence," I said, "but I think creative intelligence is simply part of the flow, which is a comforting idea. It's in the nature of our being that we understand and create, that is one with the great drama of the Universe. But it isn't God action."

"Your skepticism serves you well," he said. "Continue!"

"I have to say we are humans, and as such we cannot be objective about this being human," I said, "which, since Einstein made it respectable, is nothing to apologize for."

"Ah," he said, "accepting the inescapable reality of your humility."

"Well put," I said.

"Are you going to get to God today?" he asked quietly.

"I think maybe, but I'm not sure. I can't be sure. We can't ever be sure," I said.

"Nevertheless, proceed!" he said.

"Thank you for giving me permission to flow on through the uncertainty and the inescapable possibility of being wrong," I said.

"What's a god for?" he asked expansively.

"Compassion is the quality," I said. "That's where God comes in. I heard an author say her father told her life is pain and beauty. We don't know whether the stars feel pain or are conscious of the beauty they might perceive. We don't know if the river and the cliff feel pain as one is worn away by the other, or appreciate each other's beauty.

We think not. But pain and beauty are the emotional realities for humans. I don't know about the other objects in the flow, but for humans and maybe other creatures, it's beauty and pain."

Coyote meditated a bit, then said, "So what you come down to is that if a person or a coyote wants to find God, stay on board the planet earth and live out the beauty and pain through compassion? Is that your message up front?"

"Coyote, my friend," I said, "you have such a way with words."

He smiled complacently, then he grinned.

"You know," he said, "there's another reason for you as a professional, cynical, skeptical, sinful, compassionate clergyman not to market to those who are New Age."

"What is that?" I asked, expecting an exquisite revealing gem of an insight from my favorite local deity.

"When your New Age members waft away into the ozone, you can bet they won't pay their pledge before they leave!"

I picked up a handful of river sand and threw it in his face. He kicked some back and pretty soon we were shouting and throwing sand at each other and laughing 'til we hurt. We wrestled in the sand and rolled into the river together. We helped each other out of the cold water. He showed me how to shake. We laid in the sun and dried off. We forgot about the meaning of life for the rest of the afternoon and just watched clouds.

COYOTE WANTS TO KNOW WHY HUMANS GOT ALL THAT STUFF

 was contemplating an empty word processor screen when the door opened a crack. Coyote slipped in and hurriedly shut it behind him.

"Hey, *compadre*!" I said.

"Thank heavens you were in," he cried. "I need sanctuary!"

"Whatever for?" I asked, mixing affection and concern.

"Indian Market!" he said. "I see you're avoiding it."

"I'm maxed on Mastercard. I don't have any more display space for objets de kitsch, so I let others have my space in the crowd."

"You're wise," he said. He lay down on the sofa and shook out his tail. He fondled it forlornly. "My poor tail has been stepped on a hundred times if it's been stepped on once."

"You mean you've been on the Santa Fe Plaza *this* morning?"

"Doña Coyote insisted," he explained. "'Let's go into Santa Fe and do Indian Market,' she said. 'See what it's about. Maybe pick up a little fetish for the den.' I was against it, but she told me to be a sport. So what could I do? It's part of the mating game, right?"

"Said like a true mate," I said.

Suddenly Coyote let out a howl.

"No! No! Say it isn't so!"

"What? What?" I asked in alarm.

He held it up, and I saw the horror. It was the first Christmas catalog of the season. Coyote looked at me with anguish.

"It's August, for God's sake," he said. "Don't you humans have any sense of propriety? Have you no shame about your greed?"

I tried a feeble joke. "Well, with Christmas catalogs arriving, can Labor Day be far behind?"

"I am not in the mood to be kidded, Reverend! Your greed is killing us all! Have you humans lost all hope of becoming spiritual beings?"

With just a touch of defensiveness, I asked, "What would you suggest, O semi-divine being?"

I was offended. I think of myself as a superior example of my species, and I get defensive when judged in a discriminatory fashion by a member of another species, especially someone who is important to me spiritually.

"Other life forms don't have stuff!" he said. "You humans think you're so damn superior because you can make lots of cheap stuff. Then you have to work to pay the mortgage on a house to shelter all your belongings from God's sun and rain."

Coyote was on a roll.

"Look at this church, even! It's supposed to be a spiritual place, but you brag about what a wonderful building you've got. You impress your visitors with the courtyard and the play yard, but not with the quality of the spiritual experience that happens here. Assuming you're even willing to have a spiritual experience happen! It might detract from your worship of your glorious building!"

"Wow!" I said. "An Old Testament prophet!"

He gave me a suspicious look. "I used to be an Old Testament prophet."

"Sure," I said, "and I used to be one of the twelve apostles."

Coyote grinned and stretched and scratched himself obscenely. "So, what are we going to do, Reverend? I mean, what do we do with this human tendency to accumulate. Why do you accumulate?"

"Partly it's convenience," I said. "In California last winter I got the latest thing in vegetable scrapers. It's got this big comfortable rubberized handle; biggest improvement in vegetable scrapers in years. Makes scraping carrots so much easier."

Coyote rolled over and put his face in a pillow and howled softly. Then he sat up and said with concern, "I'll never understand you! You really seem to have possibilities for spiritual development. Maybe if you went out to Christ In The Desert Monastery and lived a simple life in all that natural beauty the way the other creatures do, you might have some peace and joy and a sense of thanksgiving instead of this awful ennui and foreboding that seems to afflict intelligent humans. Then maybe you'd have an antidote to Christmas catalogs in August."

"You're trying to tell me that the cultural anthropologists are wrong?" I asked. "What distinguishes humans from other life forms is the compulsion to collect stuff, not because we use tools?"

"Yes," he said. "Evolution made a wrong turn."

"Coyote, you have to distinguish. There are different kinds of stuff. There is good stuff and bad stuff."

"My stuff is good and your stuff is bad," he deadpanned.

"No, Coyote, there is quality stuff and—uh—non-quality stuff."

"Kitsch?"

"Ah, you might call it that."

"I don't! It's all the same to me."

"There's stuff that makes life pleasanter," I explained, "and there's stuff that makes life beautiful and pleasurable."

"Tell me about the stuff that makes life pleasurable and more beautiful."

"Oh," I said, "take the new piano in church. I grant you we could just gather and howl together, as some species I know of do. But there is a certain artistic joy and pleasure in hearing music that has been composed for and played on the piano. The piano is a human invention. None of the other animals have pianos."

Coyote nodded contemplatively. "I grant your point. I will not include the piano in my denunciation. It does have a spiritual dimension akin to the stars at night. Yes, a piano in the right hands can get the spiritual juices flowing. Name something else."

"How about the pots that artists bring to Indian Market? Pottery says something spiritual about beauty, craft, and human sharing."

He was silent. Then a tear rolled down his furry cheek.

"Damn, I have to admit I'm feeling the disadvantage of not having an opposable thumb. It's not the big brain I'm jealous of, it's the opposable thumb that allows artists to hold paint brushes and chisel stone."

"Some of us who have opposable thumbs seem to be all thumbs," I said. "So we delight in acquiring what artists have produced and taking it home to live with and be pleased by its presence in our life."

"Okay, Reverend, I'll grant that art is not to be classified as 'stuff.' But you still have too much stuff that is not spiritually enhancing."

"Does everything have to be spiritually enhancing?"

"You know it doesn't," he said. "That's why the Divine Plan includes fast cars. But the point is that while things may gladden your spirit, they have an insidious way of overwhelming the spirit and blinding you to the fact that what life is about is the fullest enjoyment of the goodness of creation. You're drowning in a spiritual malaise of greed and envy and guard-dog personalities. That's the evil side of stuff. Everyone moans about how awful it is, but nobody does anything about it, except for a few eccentrics. And even their spirituality is one of renunciation rather than a spirituality of making joyous noise unto the Lord for the beauty of a starry night—for which, believe me, the Lord is grateful. Even the Creator likes to be appreciated. Don't think your howls of ecstasy are not heard in the far reaches of the universe. Would that there were more human howls of ecstasy. The universe would be a better place."

It was my turn to be silent and thoughtful.

"So, Coyote, it seems that humans used to believe in their spiritual nature and the spiritual nature of the universe. Somehow they got to thinking that everything is material and not spiritual. They began to believe that all they could believe in are the material good things they made with their human skills. And because they believed that, they were further cut off from their spiritual side. All there was to give life meaning was more and more clever things with which to encumber their lives."

"Yes," he said. "But you've shown me that some material things do serve the purpose of expanding spiritual life. The arts and musical instruments."

"Coyote, are you suggesting that we have to discriminate which things enhance our spiritual life and which merely entertain us and make life easier and which are spiritual stones that drag us down to dreariness?"

He sat up, smiled brightly and, in the voice of a patient teacher, asked, "And how do you judge which is which?"

"By what their advertisements say about them?" I tried hopefully.

He made a rude sound.

"Ah," I said, "by checking what the neighbors have?"

Smiling broadly, he shook his head.

"Oh, I know!" I said. "By their price tag?"

Coyote was enjoying the game. "No, Reverend! Come on! You've got to have learned something from your dissolute life."

"I have lived an upright uptight life!" I said huffily.

"I know," he said, "and that's why you can't come up with the right answer. I asked what you had learned from your dissolute life, your passionate life."

"Ah!" I said. "You mean the times I just enjoyed being alive in the moment. The howls of ecstasy!"

"Exactly!" he said.

Tears came to my eyes. "What would I do without you?" I asked.

"You'd be a hell of a sad case," he said. "Now let's get down to the donut shop and see if we can't redeem the day."

So I hit Shift F-7 on my keyboard, and as we went out the door the printer was rattling off this account of a meeting of the human and the divine.

COYOTE SAYS THERE'S NO
SUCH THING AS DUMB LUCK

 stopped by the donut shop in Santa Fe to get some muffins and coffee to go. Coyote was there with some friends. He smiled and called out, "Sit down! Relax! Hang out! You look haggard from doing so much good."

"Can't do it, Coyote. I have to go to Albuquerque."

He made a face of disgust.

"There is nothing in Albuquerque you can't do without. Now sit down and enjoy our company."

"Can't do it," I said. "I'm not going for myself. I'm a substitute food-runner. I'm going to help with the food pick-up at the Roadrunner Agency and bring back some surplus food to Santa Fe for the Hunger Program. It's good work, Coyote."

He had a look of surprise and interest. "You mean there's a roadrunner food agency in Albuquerque? Maybe I'll come along!"

He gulped down his coffee, stuffed a full-grown jelly donut in one cheek and leered at the waitress. "I'm off to do good!" he said.

She gave a mock groan.

Coyote laid a hairy paw on my shoulder in the best comradely political manner, grinned expansively, and said, "Surplus roadrunners, eh? What a wonderful idea! Why go chasing them through the desert? Why spend all that money on instruments of mayhem? I'll plead poverty and the government will provide me with surplus roadkills. Thank you, my dear Reverend, for putting me onto this."

He was in the front seat before I could stop him. With the radio on to KYOT extra loud, he let his tail hang out the open window.

"You can come," I said, "but you have to help me with a sermon."

"Subject?"

"Dumb luck."

"There is no such thing as dumb luck!" Coyote said sternly.

"I have a serene parishioner who says she's been blessed with a lot of dumb luck, and she wants to know why."

He had a puzzled expression. "Why doesn't she just accept it? Why does she want to know why?"

"Intelligent humans are like that, Coyote."

We headed down Cerrillos Road toward the interstate, radio blaring, coyote tail whipping in the wind.

I thought to myself, This is dumb luck, and I love it.

"No," said Coyote firmly. "It is not dumb luck. It is grace."

One of the problems in relating to Coyote is that not even my most private thoughts are sacred. However, he is forgiving, no matter how irrational or salacious those thoughts may be.

"Grace?" I asked. "What do you mean, *grace*?"

He looked at me with disdain. "You know what grace is. It is a totally unmerited gift from God."

I thought a moment, keeping my eye on a Texas Winnebago trying to pass on the right. "You're telling me, Coyote, that there are merited gifts from God and unmerited gifts from God?"

"Of course," he said.

He blew a kiss to the woman with the cowboy hat in the Winnebago as she went past. She must have taken offense, for she blew a blast on her air horn and frightened me into the oncoming lane. I swerved back.

"See!" he explained. "There's someone who received a compliment from a god, a completely gratuitous kiss complimenting her on her poise and beauty and ability to drive a huge machine fast, and what does she do? She takes offense! Humans are so weird!"

"Maybe she didn't realize you are a god," I replied dryly.

"People think gods live off in the farthest reaches of the Universe," he said, "when actually we are everywhere."

"Which is why you think there is no such thing as dumb luck?"

"Right," he said. "It's just a little localized god activity."

"Do you recommend praying to statues in church?"

"If that's your denomination," he said. "But *you've* got *me*!"

He gave me an enthusiastic furry hug, which caused me to veer into the right lane, causing the woman in the Winnebago to sound her horn again.

"You'll get me killed, Coyote!"

"Of course," he said. "Happens to everyone. If it didn't happen to you, you'd just go on doing good forever. This way eventually you get to relax."

"I do wish I had your attitude. I can't seem to take it as it comes. I worry about it. I think it ought to be fair. I think that's why the lady asked me about dumb luck. I think she thought her dumb luck was unfair. I'm not sure she'll like it any better if I tell her it's grace."

"Why not?" Coyote asked. "Grace is a fine concept. You Universalists used to like grace. You used to say God was graceful in giving us life and beauty and a chance to make a living. You used to say all humans had to do in return was to be graceful themselves and accept God's grace and enjoy life and be good. What could be better than that?"

We were on the interstate and I relaxed.

"Coyote, I think the lady's problem is that she cares about other people. She's grateful for her own good luck, or grace, but she feels bad that so many people don't have graceful good luck."

"Well, that should simply make her more appreciative of her grace."

"It does, but she is a person of goodwill, and she wishes others could have such grace as well."

"Oh," he said, a little sadly, "that one."

"Absolutely," I said. "That one! Humans not only complain that life isn't fair when they are being dumped on. Some humans complain that life isn't fair when they are the beneficiaries of life's overflowing goodness."

Coyote squirmed in his seat and looked at the passing scenery. "Some people worry about things they shouldn't worry about," he commented morosely.

After a moment's silence, he asked in a puzzled tone, "Why can't people just accept that the world is the way it is? Nobody knows why some people are lucky and others are unlucky."

He was morosely silent. "It's just dumb luck!" he finally exclaimed.

"But you just said there's no such thing as dumb luck," I retorted. "You just said it's grace."

He sighed. Then he became happy again. His moods never last long. He looked at me with a slight grin. "The relationship between the gods and humans," said he, "is like that between a parent and a child who by some genetic fluke is smarter than the parent. Humans just ask too damn many questions of the gods, which the gods can't answer without making fools of themselves."

"Like Archibald Macleish's ditty in *J.B.*?"

"What was that?" he asked suspiciously.

"If God is good, He is not God. / If God is God, He is not good."

"What does *that* mean?" he asked, indignant.

"It means that if there is evil in the world, then God is either not all-powerful or is not good. Since there is evil in the world, God cannot be both good and all-powerful. It's a problem as old as human consciousness, as old as Job, which may be the oldest book in the Old Testament."

"That's what I mean," he said, "about humans being smarter than their creator. Until humans came along to complain, there wasn't any perception of there being evil in the world. The Universe was perfection until humans started complaining. We gods haven't had any peace and quiet since. You never heard the dinosaurs curse their fate."

"So that is the original sin of Eve and Adam?"

"Yes," he replied. "It's called the knowledge of good and evil, but really it was the human creation of the categories *good* and *evil*, which they then used to indict God and blame God for all their troubles. God told them NOT to eat of that tree! And then they blame God for all their troubles!"

A tear came to his eye and he sniffed. "And then," . . . sniff . . . "and then they call me 'trickster' and say bad things about me. When" . . . sniff . . . "all I want to do is live by the side of the road and be a friend to humans and be loved like everyone else."

He let out a long low mournful howl, but peeked out of the corner of his eye to see how I was taking it.

"Oh, for God's sake, shut up, Coyote! We love you playing tricks on people. You love it when people take you seriously and go complaining about your tricks to God. 'Why me, God, why me?' You know God's answer. 'Why not?'"

"So," he said, snapping out of it, "you go with the side of the couplet that God is not good?"

"Absolutely," I said. "Goodness is a human concept and has nothing to do with God. Which is why I'm skeptical of your position that dumb luck is really God's grace."

Coyote looked stern. "Let me get this straight," he said. "You, an ordained clergyman, are hereby doubting God's goodness?"

"I have to call 'em like I see 'em." I said.

"Like the umpire story," he said.

"Tell me the umpire story," I said.

"There were three umpires," he explained. "One umpire said 'There's balls and there's strikes, and I call 'em as they are.' The second umpire said, 'There's balls and there's strikes, and I call 'em as I see 'em.' The third umpire said, 'They ain't nothin' till I calls 'em!'"

"So what's the point?" I asked.

"The point is that you haven't progressed beyond the first stage, which is that there really are balls and strikes—good and bad—and humans call them as they are. You have progressed to the second stage, which is that there are balls and strikes—good and evil—but you call them as you see them. In other words, your prejudices and perceptions and angle of vision and state of enlightenment enter into your umpiring duties, and you can't always be clear and sure you're right. But you still think that objectively there are such things as good and bad. It's just that you can't be sure about your perception."

"And the third umpire?" I asked. "Is that a higher state of awareness?"

"Of course," he said. "I wouldn't have told the story if it weren't."

"Please draw the moral," I said as we got into Albuquerque traffic.

"The moral is that there are no such things as balls and strikes until the umpire says they are balls and strikes. It is the umpire's value judgment that makes them so."

"So you're saying," I said thoughtfully, "that the goodness or evilness of a particular happening is not something out *there*, but is a judgement by humans of the significance of an event. Which significance humans then tend to say inherently existed in the event from before it happened."

"Yes," he said.

"But," said I, "then it is indeed dumb luck and not grace, for grace implies a certain kindly attitude on the part of the deity. If not toward one human in particular, at least to humans in general."

"Typical human," he muttered. "Think they're smarter than their local deity. I have to explain everything! SLOW DOWN! There's a radar cop ahead!"

I slowed down, and with a blast of her air horn, the Winnebago driven by the woman in the cowboy hat went tearing right by into the arms of the Albuquerque police. Coyote blew her another kiss as we went by—which should be a warning to you: never pass a vehicle with a coyote tail blowing in the wind.

We turned off the interstate, loaded up with bread, and then had lunch with the happy crew of haulers. For Coyote's sake, we all pretended the chicken salad was really roadrunner. Feeling mellow, we pulled back onto the interstate and headed home for Santa Fe.

"Let's bring the instruction to a conclusion," said Coyote.

"What instruction?" I asked, feeling too mellow for theology.

"About whether God is good," he said.

"You? Good?" I asked archly.

"Not me," he said. "I'm a minor deity. It is my fate to be a trickster. I do my work well and with a certain pride. No, I'm talking about the Big Fellow, the One who told you not to eat of the apple of knowledge, but whom you disobeyed."

"You want to demonstrate that that god is good?" I asked.

"Yes."

"Then demonstrate."

"How do you feel right now?" he asked.

"Very good," I replied.

"Why?"

"Because I have done something that I think is good—helping feed people—and I am having a good time doing it." I was beginning to get the drift, and I wasn't going to fight it. I wanted to believe!

"And why do you do that?" he asked.

"Because I have had a lot of dumb luck in my life, and I am grateful for it."

"Dumb luck?" he mused.

I bit the bullet. "I've been blessed by grace in my life," I said.

"Yes," he said. "Your response indicates that in your soul, rather than in your head, you did not think it was dumb luck, because you would not react to dumb luck with a sense of having to reciprocate.

The fact that you respond to the goodness of your life with an urge to reciprocate indicates that you really are acting unconsciously as though the goodness in your life is a gift of grace rather than dumb luck. You don't have to reciprocate; it *is* a gift after all. But it draws from you a response that if you have been given unto, then you respond by giving unto others."

"And how does that demonstrate the goodness of God?" I asked.

"You people never quit, do you?" he muttered.

He went on. "Remember, you're the umpire, and they ain't nothing 'till you call them. You find what you call goodness in your life, and that calls you to respond with goodness. Like any child, you didn't follow the orders for life. You had to eat of the tree of knowledge. You outgrew God the Parent. You claim to know better than God the Parent what's good and what's evil—at least for you. Well, like any good parent, God the Parent of us all knows when to let go. So you moved out of the Garden of Eden the other animals live in and you live in your own world of good and evil."

"So," I said, "I understand all that. But how does it demonstrate the goodness of God?"

He shook his head in exasperation. "Pull over!" he ordered.

I stopped by the roadside. He opened the door.

"I've got to get away from humans!" he muttered.

From outside the car he said, "Look, you said your life was blessed, and that you understand that as grace. You said you felt an emotional need to reciprocate that grace. You said that in reciprocating that grace, in repaying the grace you had freely received without any need to repay it—but you do it anyway—you were further blessed by the company of some raffish modest one-day-a-week saints. Don't you understand that once you respond to grace by being just a little bit graceful yourself, you begin to grow in grace. The world thus is filled with grace as grace leads to further grace. That's the way God hoped it would be when you humans finally grew up. Occasionally, very occasionally, it works that way. Which is why God is good!"

"Thanks," I said.

"You're welcome," he said. He flipped his tail and was gone.

I popped Beethoven's "Hymn To Joy" in the tape deck and flew up La Bajada hill with my station wagon full of bread.

COYOTE SAYS
THERE ARE NO DULL PEOPLE

here was a loud banging on the door to my study, but before I could get to it, it burst open. A large hairy yellow-eyed, red-tongued, sharp-toothed smirk came in like an autumn storm.

"What are you doing in *here*, Reverend?" he demanded.

"Working," I said. "Or at least trying to work, but I'm not accomplishing much."

"Of course not," he said. "Your heart was out in the mountains. Why don't you get out of this stuffy hole?"

"I have to *work!*" I said.

He poked me in the ribs, hard. "No, you don't," he said. "Give me a better reason than that."

One of the troubles with being in touch with a minor deity is that he can see my secret self. There is no hiding from Coyote.

"I have to get a sermon written," I explained.

"I thought you already had a sermon you used last week in Salt Lake City."

"I do, but I have to rewrite it for the home people."

"You mean you don't tell the home people the same truths you tell the people in Salt Lake City?" He pretended to be shocked.

"My dear, divine, woolly friend," I said. "You think I have ego reasons for being inside on such a lovely day?"

"Hah!" he said. "If you were a child of your passions, if you were aware of your soul's inner need, you would be out there with the lilies of the fields and wing it on the sermon."

"Coyote, please! I have many important things to do!"

"Which makes you feel important," he jeered. "Just look in the mirror and see how important you think you are."

Instead I looked at him. He returned my gaze with merciless loving equanimity. I looked away.

"I'll retire soon enough, and then I'll be a nobody. Then I can walk with you in the glory of God's magnificent outdoors every day."

"Ah, poor man, a nobody."

If I hadn't known him for the Trickster, I might have thought he was sincerely compassionate. I decided to change the subject.

"I was watching a CNN debate in Congress, and I thought what a wonderful feeling it must be to have such power and confidence. Be honest, Coyote, wouldn't you like to be in the spotlight? Be one of the main gods? Make a difference?"

With disdain, he muttered, "Everyone's dispensable."

"True," I said. "But some people are interesting and exciting and important. Some people are unimaginative and dull and could have been dispensable from the moment of their conception."

Coyote came out of his slouch on my couch, leaned way forward, ears back and eyes like slits.

"What are you saying, Reverend? I may have to wash your mouth out with biodegradable detergent."

I said, "Well, I could never say such a thing from the pulpit, but just between you and me in the privacy of my sanctified study, isn't it not true that the majority of humans lead lives of quiet despera-tion, lives full of sound and fury, signifying nothing? In fact, maybe not even full of sound and fury. Just signifying nothing?"

He shouted, "Shame! Shame!"

"Shame, shame, my elbow," I retorted. "You can't fool me, old Trickster. I know the cynicism of the gods. You see us as entertainment, and then you discard us when you've had your fun. You just throw us away and wait for the next generation of fools you can toy with."

"Now wait a damn minute!" he protested. "We deities are good and kind and merciful and compassionate and infinitely caring. What is this cynicism about the gods you're putting out? You should be arrested for undermining people's faith. Hah! I'm going to call 911 and report you for blasphemy!"

"You don't fool me, Coyote! You know your existence is depen-dent on human belief. Without our belief, you'd just be an unincarnated lonely spirit blowing around the desert sands looking for a Moses."

"You egotist!" he shouted. "You think even the gods depend on you for our existence. Look here, you insignificant dull-witted human . . . " He sputtered out, at a loss for words.

"Oh, Coyote, we're both poor fools, gods and humans together. You're fickle and cruel, abandoning us in our need—"

He interrupted, "—and you're cruel and fickle in your worship, thinking you're self-sufficient and in control of your life. You think you don't need magic anymore. You think you don't need to worship in the desert and on the mountain."

"You!" I accused. "You couldn't care less about human pain and human stumbling in the dark. You're so all-powerful and so lacking in compassion!"

"Reverend!" he exclaimed, "what sort of reverence are you showing for the gods?"

"Unitarian Universalist reverence! I've got a tradition to uphold."

"A tradition of knocking the gods?" he asked scornfully.

"Exactly," I said. "We keep you honest. If it weren't for us and a few lonely atheists, there wouldn't be anyone to call the gods to account."

"You egotist!" he shouted.

"Damn it, it's true!" I shouted back. "If it weren't for the heretics, humans would be a bunch of bovines mooing their confusion to each other. The gods would be sickeningly unchallenged on their Mount Olympus. The nobility of heresy!"

Coyote grinned. "This is ridiculous. Gods and humans create each other. Humans created Yahweh, and that belief created a new tribe of humans who believed in their special mission. Humans created Buddha, and so they are brought to compassion by the idea of Buddha's compassion. Humans believe in the Christ, and their belief in the Christ creates human beings who serve other humans in love. You create us, and we create you. You feel the awfulness of a life without transcendence, so you create transcendence."

"And so," I said, "worshipful human activity is a dust devil in the vastness of the universe, a vain wind striving after itself."

"Not so!" he said. "That is the appearance. There is a mystery below the appearance that you and I cannot see, but we sense it when we walk in beauty or when we hear a true word spoken. It is a mystery that stirs us when we feel compassion despite our better judgment. It is a mystery that says there are no dull lives. If you could

look into each life as the Holy looks into each life and sees and understands and is filled with infinite compassion, then you would know
there are no dull lives. Every woman and every man is heroic in the
struggle to be soulful in a universe that seems barren."

"Coyote, stop it! You know I would like to believe that. But you
also know I know you are the Trickster. I refuse to believe you!"

"Fair enough," he said. "I can understand you don't trust me. But
remember, that simply means you don't trust yourself, for by your
heretical standards, you created me Trickster. You're simply saying
you are Trickster and can't be trusted!"

"So I'm left with nothing?"

"Wrong," he said. "You have a soul that tells you what is true. Everyone has a soul, the great and the dull alike. Most of the great
listen to their ego instead of to their soul. The dull have more time
to listen to their soul and find the lessons of an ordinary life. The
dull have more motivation to listen to their souls because they are
not filled with self-importance. Maybe the dull get out for a walk in
the aspens before the fall is done. Maybe they have time to listen to
other people. Maybe they get out to the farthest reaches of their
wondering and finally decide to trust the unknown and love it. Maybe
they have the wisdom to cherish the thought that the universe understands them while understanding that it might be an illusion."

"So," I said, "the wise soul finally accepts the unknown and prays
that there is love and understanding and compassion in there some-
where?"

"Just so," he said. "And so does the wise minor Trickster god
who gives thanks for the ecstasy of irony in all things divine. After
all, we gods are merely the masks the Holy wears when dealing with
humanity."

"We're not ready to see the Holy straight on?"

"Of course not," he explained. "Stories of humans burned to a crisp
by the sight of a god. Minds deranged. Not ready for the Holy. You
deal only with the masks of God. Such as me! Ta-da!"

"Let me understand," I said. "You say that the great and glamor-
ous, the people of importance and self-importance, they are not close
to the Holy?"

"As my colleague, Jesus of Nazareth remarked, 'It is harder for a rich man to get into heaven than for a camel.'"

"Camels don't get into heaven," I said.

"Of course camels get into heaven," he said. "Camels are quiet and useful and think a lot while walking across the desert. They have an unknown deep side. Jesus was simply asking, wouldn't you rather be in heaven with a nice camel than an egotistical rich man?"

I was thinking.

I asked, "You're saying the dull and useful beasts of burden are better company than the rich and famous?"

"I am saying," he explained, "that there are no dull people. There are people too caught up in their own importance to see the courage and faithfulness it takes to live an ordinary life. And there are ordinary people who sadly believe there is nothing special about being ordinary. Thus their lives seem meaningless. If I could get your attention, my important reverend friend, I would like you to go out and tell them that though they may be dull and ordinary in society's eyes, they are in fact wondrous gems of courage, love, and faith. Will you please tell them that for me?"

"Is this your opinion, or do you have it on Higher Authority?"

"I have it on the Highest Authority—on yours!"

"On mine? What do you mean, on my authority? I don't know anything. This is a major God matter."

"You dug this hole for yourself," he said. "As you say, the Holy is silent. So it is up to you as a human being who has lived more than a few years and experienced more than a few experiences—some of them better not mentioned—to dip into your experience and your feel for what life is and come to some conclusions for yourself. What do you think?"

So I thought. Thought for several moments. Let the thought come up from deep inside. I finally said, "I think there are no dull people. There are simply people whose courage we don't know. They get by on what faith and courage and love they can muster."

He asked, "And what do you think the gods think of such people?"

"It's a mystery what the gods think," I said, "but I think the gods should think highly of such people. In fact, I think the gods should be humbled by such people."

"Now wait a minute!" he protested. "Who asked your opinion on what the gods should think?"

"You did," I said. "But I would be willing to accept the gods if the gods would grant such people a sense of peace and grace in their lives."

"It seems a reasonable and humble request." He grimaced. "If this is a formal petitionary request, I will pass it on up the ladder and use all my influence to see it gets the attention of the highest levels of the divine."

"Don't strain yourself," I said with some scorn.

Then I let go of what I thought I had to do and said to him, "Coyote, will you be my guest on a drive up the mountain and a hike along a forest trail?"

"As long as I don't have to be on a leash," he said.

"Coyote, they can't *see* you!"

"I know," he said. "It makes me feel so . . . so . . . insignificant. I am beautiful, aren't I?"

The printer was happily chattering away producing this sermon as I grabbed my hat and went out into the fall's glorious sunshine. We, the children of the Earth, went off to enjoy its beauty and mystery, secure in our souls that it is right to be happy. If we could only figure out how. And if that seems dull and significant of nothing to some people, well, as Jesus said, they have their reward. The rest of us will try sneaking into heaven with the camels.

COYOTE WANTS TO
KNOW ABOUT THE MESSIAH

 came out of a meeting of the Ministerial Alliance to find the door of my truck open. A furry tail hung out.

Now what? I thought.

Of course it was himself, the Trickster, immodestly lolling across the front seats.

"I had to hot-wire it to get the radio to work," he said.

"I wish you'd have come in and gotten the keys," I groaned.

"That's a Christian church where you clerics meet," he said. "They believe in only three aspects of God, and I'm not one of them. I'm not welcome there."

"I believe in at most one," I said, "and they accept me."

"They're just being polite," he said. "Take a heretic to lunch. Why were you there? I saw your truck parked outside and thought there must be something funny happening if the Unitarian minister is at the Methodist Church. Are you up to some clergy power tricks?"

Being with a divine being who understands me, I said, "I'm tempted to express my annoyance at such a meeting, but I behave and say nothing. I bite my tongue."

"Oh," he said, all sympathy, "let's go to the donut shop and you pour your heart out to me and I'll make it all fine."

"It's all fine without your help," I said. "In fact it's usually wonderfully complacent without your help. Things get worse when you help. But in the spirit of living dangerously and joyously, let us proceed to the nutritionally impaired donut shop and flirt with sweet and fatty suicide."

As we settled in with our coffee and an assortment of sugar bombs, he said, "Tell me what universe-shattering matter of faith the local clergy have been discussing."

"You wouldn't believe it, Coyote. Only humans would believe it."

"Try me."

"They were discussing whether the Jews are guilty of killing Jesus."

"I don't believe it!" he cried.

"It's true," I said. "They feel as Christians they have been to blame for the scapegoating of Jews. They're planning some workshops with local Jews to make amends."

"How do the Jews feel about this?" he asked.

"They want to cooperate and help the Christians work out their guilt. On the other hand, I think they'd prefer to be left alone."

"And what is the Unitarian Universalist position on this important theological matter?"

"That's what I was pondering when I was coming from the meeting. I hate to seem indifferent to the pains of the Jews and the guilt of the good Christians on this matter of who killed Jesus, but it didn't really seem to involve me."

"Who do you think killed Jesus?" he asked.

"The Romans, of course."

"So why don't Christians hate Italians?" he asked.

"Italians *are* Christians, Coyote!"

"So the Christians killed Jesus?"

"No, this was before the Romans became Christian."

"So the Italians killed Jesus and then became Christians. So it all worked out. How did the Jews get involved?"

"Because the Christians didn't want to blame the Italians, I mean, the Romans. So they rewrote history to say that the Jews killed Jesus."

"This happened when?" he asked.

"About 1,960 years ago."

Coyote shook his head and signalled for more donuts. "I would think they could find more contemporary problems to face." he commented.

"I think it's a long-running family argument. Christians and Jews share this idea that either the Messiah has come or the Messiah is going to come. The Jews think the Messiah hasn't come yet, which offends the Christians, who think the Jew, Jesus, was the Messiah. This Christian claim offends the Jews who think it isn't anyone else's business whether their Messiah has come or not. If Jesus just hadn't been a Jew, the Jews would still be an obscure minor sect in the spectrum of the world's religion with a belief that the Messiah is coming sometime. Lots of religions believe that a messiah figure is coming, so all the Jews would rate is a footnote in comparative religions if it weren't for their role in Christianity."

"So what's a messiah?" he asked.

I opened my *Oxford Dictionary of the Christian Church*. Even though it's 1,500 pages, I always carry it with me in case some smart-aleck wants to see if she can catch me uninformed.

"Let's see," I said, "Messiah . . . ah, here it is! 'A person invested by God with special powers and functions.'"

"Like me," he said.

"No, not like you! A person! It has to do with a glorious king or queen who is going to reign as monarch of a kingdom of righteousness. The Jews thought it would be a kingdom on earth from the lineage of their glorious King David. They thought all the other kingdoms and tribes would recognize the superiority of their divinely appointed king. The trouble, of course, is that all monarchs claim to be anointed by God, even the British royal family. The Christians preempted the imagery and said Jesus was the Messiah. But somebody killed him. The Greek word for 'messiah' is transliterated into English as 'Christ'; Jesus the Christ. Someone killed him, but he returned from the grave. So his real kingdom is a spiritual kingdom, not a kingdom of this world."

Coyote leaned over the counter, picked up the coffee pot and filled both our cups. The waitress rolled her eyes. Coyote stuck out his tongue at her. They both giggled. I thought donut shops are not the place for serious theological matters.

"If it was all spiritual, why was Jesus killed?" Coyote asked.

"Jesus was killed by the Romans because they thought he was a troublemaker who would upset the Pax Romana based on free trade, low wages, and imperial troops."

"Like the international corporations and free trade?"

"Exactly."

He shook his head. "But if the Kingdom of Jesus is spiritual, what difference does it make to the Pax Romana or the international business community?"

"It shouldn't make any difference," I explained. "Jesus is even reputed to have said, 'Render unto the corporations what belongs to the corporations, and render unto God what is God's.'"

"Sounds like good Republican doctrine to me," he said.

"It would seem that way," I said, "but you don't understand human nature. There is one great commandment of the human ego: 'thou shalt have no king before me; thou shalt have no loyalty higher than the corporation.'"

"And spiritual loyalty to God is considered in conflict with human ego?" he asked.

I quoted Scripture to him: "What doth the Lord require of thee, but to do justice, to love mercy, and to walk humbly with thy God?"

He nodded thoughtfully, gazing at the sludge in his coffee cup. "So kings and corporations don't like that commandment?"

I said, "They don't like justice; they don't like mercy; and they don't like walking humbly. They like power and winning."

"So you're saying that the world of empire and the world of the spirit are in conflict."

"Ninety-eight percent of the time through human history they have been."

"What about the other two percent?" he asked.

"Well, I left two percent for hope and the occasional enlightened rich person who might manage to squeeze through the eye of the needle and operate in the spiritual kingdom."

"But why the Messiah?" he asked.

"Cheap grace," I said. "People were wanting the hard work done for them. They wanted Jesus to die and go to hell for them, and then rise up and be transformed and take them all with him as loyal subjects. Immensely popular idea. And you can understand it. Most people find the spiritual path too much in conflict with the daily demands of plain surviving, so they would prefer to have a Messiah do the hard work for them and just say, 'Yeah, I believe' and get an automatic ticket to spiritual paradise."

Coyote hunched up close to me and said in a low voice into my good ear, "Well, why not? It doesn't do any harm to believe that, does it? It makes people happier. No one's ever going to know on this earth whether they were right or wrong. Why not believe in the Messiah and enjoy life?"

I looked him straight in the yellow of his eyes and replied, "Because if I believed in the Messiah, I wouldn't believe in you. It's more fun to believe in you!"

He blushed under his fur . . . I can tell. "I'm flattered," he said. "But the Messiah can offer you so much more than I can."

"No," I said. "You can offer me more than the Messiah. The Messiah offers to do it for me. One answer fits all humans. You, my minor divinity friend, offer me a dialogue, an opportunity to discover for myself what my meanings are."

"For example," he prompted.

"For example, such a homely thing as sitting here enjoying caffienated sludge and sugar bombs. Does one enjoy life and tempt premature coronary occlusions? Or does one go for longevity, albeit sensible longevity? That is a question of life's meaning, of life's quality. To sit in an undistinguished donut shop considering ephemeral spiritual truths or sit at an oak desk figuring ways to avoid paying one's fair share of taxes for the common good. I would rather not leave such matters, minor as they are, to the Messiah. I would rather work them out for myself, work out my spiritual destiny in terms of my own life experience in all its uniqueness and commonality."

"Do justice, love mercy, and walk humbly with thy God?" he quoted back to me.

"All except the walking humbly with my God." I said.

"What?" he said, shocked. "You don't want to walk humbly with thy God?"

"No," I said, "I want to sit humbly with my god in a donut shop and drink coffee and discuss such things as whether we need a messiah."

He grinned and all his coyote teeth shone and his yellow eyes seemed to sizzle with light. He put his paw on my shoulder and said, "And maybe take your god in your humble four-wheel drive road-runner down to the Rio Grande and go skinny-dipping?"

"Yeah!" I said, "we can leave the justice and mercy for tomorrow."

"Right!" he said. He paused, then added, "That justice and mercy is hard work! You sure you wouldn't like a god to take care of it for you?"

"And miss the fun?" I said. "Justice and mercy are what create the human soul!"

"And skinny-dipping humbly with thy God," he said.

I didn't answer that. I was sure it would be a humbling experience.

A PLEDGE CALL ON
WILEY AND DOÑA COYOTE

 never make pledge calls. The chair of the church pledge drive said I had to make this one. The board of trustees was worried about the pledge increases necessary to run the church, so the chair pledge of the drive assured them he would ask me to get a little divine help. He was so excited by the idea of tapping the divine abundance that he wanted to come along and help. I thought it needed a delicate touch.

I got Doña Coyote on the telepathic Internet, and as always she regarded me with suspicion. I said I needed to talk to Coyote. She put him on, but I could hear her say, "It's that no-good reverend! You be careful what you agree to."

I said I wanted to come over and pay a call on himself and Doña Coyote. He was silent. Then in a voice filled with suspicion, he asked, "What about?"

"Oh," I said nonchalantly, "about the annual canvass at the church."

"You want to come here?" he asked.

I could hear alarm in his voice. In the background I could hear Doña screaming: "He can't come here! We don't have a Bible! We have nothing to serve him but leftover mice and moles."

"Ah, uh, well," stammered Coyote. "No!" he finally said. "I don't think so. It would be awfully far for you to come way out here, and I wouldn't want you getting your suit dirty coming down in our burrow. Besides the light isn't very good in here. I hate to say it, but I just don't think—"

"Well," I interrupted, "how about meeting me at the donut shop."

"Yes, yes," he said. "Excellent idea! I'll be there right away!"

"I want Doña to come, too."

"You want Doña to come, too?" he asked suspiciously. "Why do you want Doña to come?"

"I want to talk to you both." I said.

"Wait a minute."

Telepathically I could hear him whisper to Doña, "He wants you to come, too."

I heard her whisper back, "What's he up to?"

Coyote whispered, "I don't know, but it's free donuts."

Doña whispered, "Well, okay, but let me get my coat brushed first."

So ten minutes later I got to the donut shop and they materialized. They were both very formal and polite and cheerful and wanted to know what sort of day I was having, and all that. "Sniffing" we call it.

I ordered a couple dozen cream-filled and three coffees. I opened with the official canvass gambit: "So, what's the church mean to you guys?"

"It's fun!" said Coyote.

"It's a menace," said Doña Coyote.

I had the feeling I was in for a hard sale.

"Tell me what's wrong," I asked Doña.

"It's the minister," she said, cool as anything.

I was determined not to lose it.

"You have a problem with the minister?" I reflected.

"He leads coyotes into temptation and irresponsibility and threatens them with cardiac arrest."

She was clearly enjoying herself. She needed to get her feelings aired. Coyote seemed to be in a world of his own. No help from him!

"Interesting you should say that, Doña Coyote," I said. "My wife says the same thing about Coyote."

She allowed herself a wan smile. "Well, we're both right," she said. "I admit he's probably a bad influence on you. You are a bad influence on each other."

"But we do have fun together," I said. "I'm much more cheerful around the house after I've been with Coyote."

"Oh," she said, relaxing. "You may be right. Maybe it's really harmless. However, I've noticed there's a questioning tone when he howls his praises to creation after he's been with you."

"Affirming your doubts means you have a strong faith!" I said in my best cheerful professional clergy manner.

"Not the way I was brought up," she retorted. Then she said, "So why did you invite us here to ply us with sugar bombs?"

And to show she had no ill will, she scarfed down two in one bite. I was glad to see that for all her good upbringing, Doña could still be a coyote.

"Oh," I said as innocently as possible, "everyone is upping their pledge this year to pay for better music and better computers. I thought that perhaps since the church is such a large part of your life, you might want to contribute from your divine providence."

Coyote looked at me skeptically. "How much are you increasing your pledge?"

"Fifteen percent," I said, "$300."

I could see him calculating. I expected to see the numbers roll up in his eyes like a one-armed bandit.

"I'm impressed," he said. "Does that include donuts for me?"

"Donuts are extra," I said.

Coyote looked at Doña. They exchanged a husband-wife sort of look, and Coyote said, "Okay, we'll match you!"

"Wow!" I said. "That's wonderful!"

They laughed, ate up the last of the donuts, drained their coffee cups, thanked me, and started to fade. Just at the last, I heard Doña Coyote's voice whispering, "Fifteen percent of nothing is nothing!"

Then there was a hair-raising dual hilarious howl.

I paid the bill and left a tip. I wondered how I was going to tell the pledge chair what happened. I bet they won't let me canvass anymore!

Hey, that's too bad!

COYOTE LOVES TO SING!

oyote and I were having something unhealthy at Dunkin' Donuts, just a little happy male-bonding, you know. I mentioned to him that a choir from Oklahoma was coming to visit.

"A people choir?" he asked.

"Of course it's a people choir!" I said. "What other kind of choirs are there?"

He looked down his nose at me, which for a coyote is a long look. "I'll have you know that Tulsa is the home of a world-famous coyote choir."

"A coyote choir?" I asked.

I'm afraid my species-ism showed. I try not to be species-ist, but every now and then the underlying species-ism of all humans shows, things like being condescending to dogs and eating hamburgers.

"Don't tell me you have never heard a coyote choir?" he asked, rather haughtily.

"As a matter of fact I have," I replied. "It was in the Pecos mountains. In the middle of the night. I came up and out of my sleeping bag as though it was the end of the world and Gabriel was blowing his horn."

"Beautiful, no?" he smiled.

"It sounded more like the ritual murder of babies. I was moved by the terror of it rather than the beauty of it."

"You have no taste!" he said, offended.

"I like you and I like donuts," I said, trying to establish our camaraderie again.

"I mean musical taste!" he said. "Everyone likes donuts and me. Musical taste is a sign of culture, which is why Tulsa is considered such a cultured place."

"Because of the choir at All Souls Unitarian Church?" I asked.

"No!" he said. "Because of the coyote choir!"

"Do they perform in public?" I asked, still amazed that Tulsa was famed for its coyote choir.

"Well, they don't perform in concerts where people pay admission, if that's what you mean. Coyotes are not considered socially acceptable by the better people in Tulsa. It would be hard to get a paying audience. No," he went on, "Coyote choirs perform for the love of it. They love to sing the good old coyote hymns. They love to hear their voices blending. They love keeping a sharp eye out for the little tricks the conductor likes to play on them, changing the tempo of the yaps in the middle of a chorus, bringing in the bass howlers right when the sopranos are doing a very delicate little yipping trill. It's sort of jazz yelping, and it's music to furry ears."

"Have you heard them?"

"Oh, yes, Doña Coyote and I have been to Tulsa many times for the annual howl off at the second full moon of summer. And the Tulsa Howlers and Yelpers, T-H-Y, love getting out of Tulsa and coming to New Mexico. That was a THY practice session that woke you up that night in the Pecos."

"It was really very beautiful once I got over my fright! The moon was full. The valleys were full of mist. It made a truly unearthly experience to come suddenly awake, startled awake by angelic music, seeing moonlight through the mist. Truly transcendent! I doubt there's any human music that could compete."

"Well," he said, "you may be lacking in taste, but I think you might be trained to appreciate good music after all."

"Would you like to come over Friday and hear the children's choirs from Tulsa's All Souls Unitarian Church?" I asked.

He looked at me, apparently unsure what to say. "Will there be food?" he asked.

"Of course," I said. "You know Unitarian Universalists have given up everything ecclesiastical except potluck suppers."

"You're not going to ask the congregation to sing, are you?"

"What's wrong with the congregation's singing?" I asked. It was my turn to be indignant!

He said, "There is no understanding taste, but to my furry ears it sounds like yelps and howls and babies being murdered."

"Coyote!" I said. "That is unkind! Our singing is called making a joyful noise unto the Lord!"

He snickered. "And have you inquired of the Lord whether She joyfully listens?"

I smiled. "We know that our Universalist Goddess understands and forgives all."

"Lucky for you!" he said.

I'm sure he was joking.

I signalled the waitress for another round of donuts and coffee. Then the same thought occurred to both of us. He said it first, "It doesn't matter whether anyone listens. It only matters that we sing!"

COYOTE WANTS TO KNOW
WHY EVERYONE CAN'T AGREE

cashed a check and went to the donut shop. I ordered a coffee and a bran muffin.

"Something for him?" the waitress asked.

"No," I said, "I need to be alone."

She came back with my bran muffin and a stack of sugary donuts. Coyote materialized on the stool next to me.

"Nice try," he said. "It didn't work."

"What have you got on the waitress?" I asked.

"A gentleman never tells," he said.

He popped three cream-filled donuts into his mouth, and through the sugar and coffee managed to say with a nasty smile, "Having sermon troubles?"

"No! No! I am quite capable of writing my own sermons."

"Wouldn't be as good as if I were helping you."

"I can't afford your help every week," I said.

But I imagined being all alone at the word processor and thought, What the hell! I signaled the waitress for a lemon-filled and a coffee refill. Wallow in camaraderie, I thought. Accept the universe's help.

I said, "I have a problem. Our Unitarian Universalist big offices say we need more people of color, more ethnic variety, more lifestyle diversity. We're too much an Anglo elitist intelligence-based religious community."

Coyote looked mystified. "I thought that's what everyone aspired to become. Except me, of course. I have no wish to become an Anglo elitist intelligent human being."

"Why not?" I asked. I was surprised and surprised to realize I was surprised.

"You kidding?" he said. "I thought you were spiritually advanced enough to know that that's something you work *out* of, not *into*."

"I'm ambivalent," I said, suddenly embarrassed by my new L. L. Bean button-down tattersall shirt.

"I don't know why I keep trying with you," he said in the exasperated tone of a parent to a thirteen year old. "You seem so . . . "

"Full of unrealized potential?" I finished for him.

"Yes!" he said. "Exactly! I have high hopes for you, and then you relapse into this infantile behavior, into this mind-limiting classist racist behavior. Can't you get free of your classist racist intellectual trip?"

"This feels good and familiar," I said. "Yes, the security of feeling guilty about who I am!"

He screamed! Everyone in the donut shop looked up.

"No! No! No! Your guilt is the mark of your elitism. Get rid of your classism and racism and intellectual elitism and you will get rid of the guilt that goes with it!"

Dear God, I prayed, deliver me from a politically correct coyote.

He heard what I was praying. He began to whisper, and the other customers went back to sleep with the want ads in front of them.

"I am not a politically correct coyote. That is human folly. You are the one who is worried about being politically correct. I am trying to get you free to become a spiritual being and accept everyone else as a spiritual being."

"I don't want to be a spiritual being, Coyote. I just want to drink coffee and dunk donuts and have fun with my friends."

"Ah," he said, "I'm reassured. That's what I call being a spiritual being."

"Okay," I said. "If that's what a spiritual being is, I'll be one. Are you one, too?"

"Of course. How could you ever doubt it? We wouldn't be having this conversation here if we weren't both spiritual beings. You have come a long way from your liberal, elitist, white-male certainties. It has allowed you to see other ways of being."

I hunger for his approval, which annoys me. Elitist white males are not supposed to pander for the approval of the gods.

So I said, "You think I'm man enough to accept diversity? You think I'm getting more open?"

"You're a swinging door," he replied. "Flip-flop, flip-flop. Open, closed, open, closed."

"That's reality spiritually," I said. "Now you see it, now you don't."

He muttered, "I'm glad that's understood!"

I was feeling better, what with sugar and caffeine and a grudging divine approval. I said, "I'm beginning to think diversity might not be too bad. As long as there's not too much of it."

Coyote stared at himself in the back-bar mirror, summoning strength to go on with his spiritual tutoring. "I'm against diversity," he said.

I was confused. "But I thought you liked the give-and-take, the howl-and-growl."

"I think life would be easier if everyone agreed with me," he said.

"Easier for whom?" I asked.

He looked down his snout at me as if wondering why I was too stupid to see the obvious. "Easier for me," he said.

"But what if you were wrong? Would you want everyone to agree with you?"

He thought about that for a minute, had a sip of coffee, and nodded—Yes. "They could just as easily agree I'm right, and then we'd all be right."

He grinned his toothy grin, and I could see there were occasions when it would be wise to agree with Coyote even when you knew he was wrong.

I said, "But suppose it isn't clear who's right?"

"Precisely my point," he said. "Such differences lead to arguments and committee meetings and funding studies and listening politely to other people's points of view. A lot of time gets wasted that could be spent out in the desert chasing a fat healthy rabbit. Diversity is a drag. No one really likes it."

"I can't believe you're saying this, Coyote. What about all the fun arguments we've had over the years? What about all the insights we've offered each other?"

He looked at me coldly. "I offered you insights. You never offered me any. You are a parish minister and I am a minor deity. There is such a thing as rank, and it should be respected."

"Coyote, *compadre*, I deeply respect your vast wisdom, but we *have* discussed certain matters that humans know about which the gods do not experience: tragedy, dying, and the limits of space and time.You're a minor deity, but you've never dealt with living a life on insufficient information."

"You think humans have information we gods don't have?" he asked archly.

"Of course!" I replied. "Humans have to make their own meaning. That's how they discover that the work of love leads to joy and that every day spent angry is time lost for being happy."

"That's profound," he said. "You make that up?"

"It's a local Hispanic proverb," I said.

Coyote licked crumbs off his fur and then observed, "You've got to admit that if everyone were of the same mind, it would make for efficiency and peace. Don't efficiency and peace count for something?"

"Cultures seem to think so," I said. "'Conformity' it's called. Pressures and sanctions to get everyone thinking the same way. But not between friends. If you can't get to the real soul differences and accept them joyously, then it isn't a real relationship. Everybody's got to have a few soul relationships to feel real and be happy."

"So," he said, "personal relationships flourish on diversity, but social relationships encourage conformity. Doesn't that confuse people?"

I looked thoughtfully into my coffee cup. "That's the way it used to be. That's the way it pretty much still is. But it's changing. It's not the way it's going to be."

He was surprised. "Things are changing?"

"We think so," I said. "People used to believe that answers came down from the top. Now we're beginning to think answers come up from the bottom."

"Careful," he said. "Sounds like heresy again."

"I'm a Unitarian Universalist minister," I said. "I'm paid to be a heretic."

"Just checking. Sometimes you're so straight I think you're in danger of becoming orthodox."

I ignored him and said, "The advantages of diversity aren't an untried idea. People who live in organizations that honor diversity seem to come closer to the truth, on the whole, than organizations that get their truth from the top down. I know that's bitter for the deities, but it's true."

He challenged me. "Example!"

"Our little church," I said. "It's a fairly pure democracy. Everyone who wants to has her or his say. We come to consensus. When we have consensus we act. And we get things done because everyone feels they own a part of it. People think of something that seems like a good idea, they just bring it up. We're open to the possibility of doing better. We value and honor our critics. However, we expect them to help implement their criticism. No sideline critics."

He said, "But you don't get out a product. You don't have to be efficient."

"It works for organizations getting out a product, too. They are learning to listen to their customers. But you're right, we're in the business of giving people meaning in their lives. The old model is that people give their life to some grander cause in which decisions are made by the elite. They end up with a certificate of thanks for their room in the retirement center. Our model is that we honor people in our community, not through giving up life to a grand cause, but through honoring specialness, uniqueness, and experiential insights, our personal slant we've gained from living a life."

"No place for an impatient leader, eh?"

"No," I said, a little ruefully. "There's a lot of patience and listening needed to be a leader of today's human beings."

He said, "But it sure pays off, doesn't it?"

I was taken by surprise. "How do you mean?"

"Why," he said, "it gives you hope. All these smart people with different ideas just bubbling up. New ideas, new ways of trying things. Women with ideas about how to run the world. People with not much gold, but a lot of soul. People who feel secure enough to try being free and honest. People of color with a story to tell. Clever. And you know what?"

"What?" I asked.

"They all got a little coyote in 'em. That's what makes it so much fun."

With that he spun twice on the stool and disappeared.

I paid up and headed back to the word processor. I thought, we may have a long way to go to get human diversity in our little congregation, but at least we've got divinity diversity. We have a hairy-faced, yellow-eyed Trickster, some re-emergent goddesses, and a genial retired God the Father. Maybe the human diversity will follow.

COYOTE GOES ON RETREAT

oyote hadn't been around. I hadn't seen him at the donut shop. I hadn't seen him on the path. He hadn't jumped in the truck. I missed him. I missed his cynicism, his sarcasm. I missed his caring, his forgiving nature. I missed his raunchiness, his sentimentality. I was stuck with myself.

I went out to the overlook at Santa Cruz Lake and looked over. Beautiful day. Magnificent scenery. That's nice, I thought.

But as I drove away, a road I hadn't seen before appeared. I took it.

No sooner had I shifted into four-wheel drive when a familiar figure raced from behind a piñon tree and jumped in the front seat.

"God, I'm hungry!" he said. "What did you bring to eat?"

He rummaged through my backseat filing system sending papers flying every which way.

"I didn't know you were going to be here," I said. "And couldn't you say 'hello' before you start destroying things?"

"Hello," he said. "Isn't there anything to eat in this truck? I've only had one small rodent this whole morning."

I pulled some granola out of my emergency supplies. He looked gratified and disgusted at the same time.

"Oh, Coyote, come on. We'll go into town and get you a pie."

"Can't do that," he said. "On retreat."

"Retreat? What's that?" I asked.

"A spiritual retreat," he said archly. "Surely as a clergyperson, you know what a retreat is."

"I know what a retreat is, but I never expected to find you on one."

"A time for spiritual renewal." He paused. "I *am* a spiritual being, therefore I occasionally need spiritual renewing."

"Me too," I said happily. "That's why I'm out here."

"Driving around in a truck with the stereo and air-conditioning on is not my idea of spiritual renewal."

I was defensive. "I don't have the stereo on, and the windows are open."

"Geez," he said. "If it was my truck, I'd have the stereo and the air-conditioning on and some beer in the cooler and a good supply of Danish. You may be a spiritual being, too, but you don't know how to have fun."

"You've been out in the desert too long," I said.

He sighed. "That's true. One can be spiritual only so long, and then one has to get back to the world of materialism."

"What do you do on a spiritual retreat?" I asked.

He gave me a suspicious look. "I'll never tell."

"But you're my spirit guide," I protested. "You're supposed to be helping me attain a greater and purer spirituality. I need you as my role model."

We had entered a narrow canyon with a sandy bottom. I stopped and shifted to low range. We eased through a right angle turn in a canyon about as wide as the truck. I was anxious about whether there would be a place to turn around.

Coyote of course knew what I was thinking.

He said, "You think you're getting out into the beautiful outdoors, but your mind is really on this piece of machinery and getting it out without badly denting it. You're not in a spiritual place, although you kid yourself that you are. You could have walked down this canyon. Then you might have been in touch with Mother Earth."

"You're right," I said. "Shall we get out and walk?"

"No," he said. "This is fun."

Which was fine with me. I was willing to settle for fun and be spiritual another day.

Sounding philosophical, he continued, "Creatures unconsciously worship everyday That's what it means to be a spiritual being. When your energy is directed to maneuvering this wonderful piece of machinery through this canyon, your spirit is concerned with your skill. You're testing whether you can do what you will yourself to do. Thus you are worshipping; worshipping human ingenuity—your own and that of the people who made this wonderful vehicle, the economic system that supplied it to you and provide you the leisure to be out tromping the flora of the desert."

"Are you accusing me of being a materialist?"

"I'm not accusing you," he explained. "You *are* a materialist. Humans are all materialists. At least the healthy ones are. They have a healthy joy at what they have created. They are filled with wonder at their collective brilliance, sometimes even dazzled by it. Fortunately you are not one of the latter, or I would not hang out with you. But when you do your materialism with a joyful happy heart, you are worshipping that skillful part of being human."

"I don't think I'm supposed to say that in church, Coyote."

"Maybe that's why so many people of good sense have given up going to church," he theorized. "They know what is good and true and beautiful. A lot of what is good and true and beautiful doesn't get acknowledged in church. For instance, that new piano in your church. I think it's lovely you have a piano as an object of worship, to venerate and play upon and listen to. You have a pulpit, the wonder of the spoken word. And a piano, the wonder of music that is beyond words."

I said, "In the family I grew up in, Sunday morning consisted of listening to classical music, reading *The New York Times*, and being together as a family."

"See?" he said. "No wonder you turned out so well! Culture and information and love. What could be more gloriously human? Sounds like true worship."

We came around a tight bend. There was Santa Cruz Lake and a tiny beach with some cottonwoods just beginning to bud. We got out and felt the sand between our toes.

"Are you telling me," I asked, "that humans should worship humaness? What about all that is good and true and beautiful that is not human or human-created?"

"That," said he, "is the reason for coming out here on retreat. There are other realities than the human reality going on. Humans need to acknowledge this fact in their worship life if they are to be realistic, healthy, wise, and good as humans. And," he added as an afterthought, "so do other creatures. But it's easier for other creatures to concentrate on the beauty that surrounds them, because they don't have the distractions humans have, such as special vehicles for recreation. Indeed, they have to be careful not to be squashed by a recreational vehicle. You can't blame them for thinking those machines are demonic."

"All in your point of view," I replied. "What about the demonic, Coyote? There seems to be a lot of it around. Do we venerate the demonic?"

"You do," he said. "We don't. The demonic is a human invention that the gods do not understand. Some humans just seem to enjoy inflicting pain. Perhaps because they had pain inflicted on them. Non-humans cause pain in the course of working out their fate, but there doesn't seem to be the enjoyment of cruelty that marks some humans."

"I knew a man once who enjoyed inflicting and receiving pain. Said it made him feel alive. His wife divorced him."

"Amazing," said Coyote. "But I guess you can understand that if pain given and received made him feel alive, then that's what he would worship. He would create a theology that pain is life, so pain is good. So let's get out and do it."

"What about God, Coyote? Many people think worship has to do with God. They think humans should sit in rows where God is up front in the church. If you want to get close to God, kneel at the rail that separates us from God. Maybe you'll be given a little piece of God."

"That's another thing the gods don't understand," he said. "Why people want to separate themselves from the gods. Why do they make up these stories that the gods are so distant? Here we are, you a well-brought-up human and me a minor deity. We're having a good time with sand between our toes discussing high-level stuff. We're basking in the spring sunshine and the phone can't find us. Why do humans want to get apart from the gods? At least think of us, if you can't think of yourselves. Why would we want to live in a little box in an empty dark church? Why would we want to be available to you humans one day a week for an hour? We love you. What do you expect us to do with the rest of our time? Think about someone besides yourself, for God's sake!"

Coyote was gesticulating and working himself up into froth. We sat quietly while he collected himself. I meditated on his words.

"Of course we gods have our faults," he added. "If you want perfection, hang out with some rocks. But if you're a spiritual being, what's wrong with talking to the gods?"

"You do it too much, you can get incarcerated," I said.

"You seem to get away with it," he deadpanned.

"I have a special license," I said.

"You know," he said, "you're not entirely free of the One God Theory. I wish I could break you of that. The universe was not all plannned and executed by one Supreme Mind. Nor is there One God micro-managing your life and mine. The pagan polytheists had the right idea. They found the god-spirit everywhere. They understand the little demons that hide in your truck and make alarming moaning sounds. Spirits reside in the lake, which is why you come here. The world used to be invested with magic. You honored the rain. Now you complain about the rain. You forget there are all these little gods you can access by creating a work of art or sitting quietly by yourself. You made One God and put him in a church so you could control him! You're a spiritual being, not a rock!"

A voice cried in the wilderness, "Hey, we got feelings, too."

Coyote looked around, spooked. "What was that?"

"Just a rock," I said.

He looked at me, then said admiringly, "You've been taking up ventriloquism."

"Not me," I said. "Apparently you offended a rock by implying they aren't spiritual."

Coyote stared at me and then turned inward. After a moment, he stood and faced the small canyon and addressed the rocky defile: "My apologies," he said.

A voice cried again, "No offense. We just wanted to raise your consciousness."

"See?" said Coyote to me. "You stay open, you learn something new everyday. I now have a new respect for the spirituality of rocks. I was blind, but now I see!"

"I think we may have an ethical problem, Coyote. There's no way we're going to get out of this canyon without driving over a lot of rocks."

"Maybe," he mused, "we should think of it as helping them to loosen themselves from their stationary state; help them to travel and see the world."

There was no response from the rocks, so we took it as permission to pass. After all, mountains are in motion. It's just that they move very slowly. And need help.

As we got back in the truck, he said, "Your Mother has been good to you. Have you been good to her?"

"I came out here to visit with her. I found the lake and the rocks, and you and I had a spiritually refreshing time. I have some good things to say about our Mother when I get back to the people in church."

"I like that," he said. "I'm sure she appreciates it. Just as long as you don't try to keep God in a box."

"I assure you," I said. "You'll never find God in a box in a Unitarian Universalist church."

"Fine!" he said. "Then let's try to get this minor god a little counterspace in a donut shop. This spiritual retreat has made me ravenous."

I slipped the clutch and, believe it or not, several large boulders made room for us to get through as we left the fissure in Mother Earth.

At the communion rail, Coyote raised his coffee cup and said, "Thank god for donuts."

"You're welcome," I said.

He made an obscene gesture with his tail, which I cannot repeat, since, alas, I do not have a tail to tell.

YOU BETTER LOOK OUT!
COYOTE'S COMING DOWN
YOUR CHIMNEY TO STEAL YOUR SOCKS

here was snow in the parking lot of the supermarket, so I shifted into four-wheel drive. I found a place between a new Range Rover and a pickup in primer. I nodded to the Salvation Army Santa and picked up some holiday necessities. As I exited, the Salvation Army Santa stuck his foot out and tripped me. I landed in the slush and salt and cinders. I sat up, wondering what attorney would take on a Salvation Army Santa.

"What in the name of Christmas did you do that for?"

"'Cause you're a cheapskate," said Santa.

The voice was familiar. The yellow eyes were familiar.

"I thought charity was supposed to be voluntary," I said, getting up and brushing myself as best I could. "I'm going to call an officer of the law and have you incarcerated for fraud."

"Oh, I'm not trying to fool you," said Coyote. "I'm trying to help some rich sucker work out his codependency. I'm in quest of the impulsive $100 bill. You're not even small change, cheapskate. Keep moving!"

"You're an evil spirit," I said. "A fraud trading on guilt and human kindness."

"I am not an evil spirit. I am merely a tricky spirit. I am the spirit of Christmas ambiguity. I am the light touch in the heaviness of the winter solstice."

"How're you doing?"

I looked in his pail. A New York subway token and some beads from Taiwan.

"Not good," he said.

"Location is everything," I said.

"I tried the Inn at Loretto," he said, "but a lady wanted to buy me. She said 'Oh, look at the cute coyote in a Santa suit' and started feeling for my price tag. She got rather personal. I growled at her."

"Get out of that outfit. I'll get some biscochitos from the bakery, and we'll celebrate Advent."

A few minutes later, loaded with sweets and coffee, we slid into traffic. I told him the story of how the Grinch stole Christmas. Coyote was all approval until I got to the part where the Grinch gave all the presents back to the people of Whoville. He shook his head.

"Really stupid!" he said.

"It's the whole point of the story," I said.

"I know," he said, "but it's still stupid."

"The point of Christmas is giving, Coyote!"

"Hah! The point of Christmas is *getting*. There is joy in the nation because the cash registers are ringing. The merchants in the mall aren't giving the stuff away. They're selling it. You are still influenced by the naive liberalism of your youth."

"Coyote, the Grinch stole the presents. He was a mean, nasty, selfish, small-hearted, cynical—"

"Realist," he finished.

"You stupid flea bag," I retorted. "Christmas is about love and light in the darkness and grace and the goodness and happiness of being human."

"Hey, hey," he said. "Let's keep a sense of humor about human goodness. Let's not take goodwill and peace so seriously we have a stroke."

I was ready to invite him out of the truck—at speed.

"Coyote, Christmas is to remind us there is a warmer human side, that we aren't meant to live just on cynicism."

"But you have to admit it's ambiguous," he replied. "It may not be enough to be a cynic, but if you don't lock your chimney, someone's going to come down it and steal your socks."

I was getting over it. Sugar and caffeine do it for me.

"You know, Coyote, I wonder about the Grinch. All those years he was in his cold cave hating the fun in Whoville. Now I can understand a Grinch not taking part in the fun and joy of Christmas. That's his right. Stay home and sulk. But something changed the Grinch into someone who had to actively interfere with other people's fun. What changed him for the worse, Coyote? Dr. Seuss never says why he chose this particular time to steal the toys."

Coyote drained his cup and threw it into the backseat with my papers.

"Not much is known of the psychology of Grinches," he said.

"There are enough of them," I said. "You'd think they would have been studied."

"There are two reasons Grinches haven't been studied," he said. "The first is that they are so dull and unpleasant no one can stand to interview them. Researchers have left them to revel in their misery."

"What is the other reason?"

"Grinches are so sure that they're right in their cynicism that they intimidate anyone who studies them. Their cynicism is catching. No amount of carols or crèches or stars can get past their cynicism and convince them that caring and fun are real."

"I suppose Grinches have a point," I said. "Even though the people of Whoville had a better time than the Grinch, they did seem a little sickening sweet. What's the solution to this ambiguity?"

"Love and larceny," he said.

"Love and larceny?" I repeated, dumbly. "Explain please, dear superior spiritual being."

"You have to understand," he said patiently, "that to be a happy human you have to accept the reality of love and the reality of larceny. Most humans get involved in one or the other and forget the other one. Those involved in larceny forget about love. Those who commit to love are made nervous by the larcenous impulses they have. Love *and* larceny are the human condition. The divine condition, too, if that helps."

"I don't get it," I said.

"Oh, you get it. You just can't admit you get it. Christmas is about love. It's also about larceny, a gentle sort of legalized larceny, a socially approved expression of greed. What am I gonna get? It is the most ambiguous of holidays, and thus it is the truest of holidays. It's only people like the Grinch who refuse to accept the ambiguity who don't get it."

"Why can't it always be nice and warm like Whoville," I asked, with just a hint of a whine.

Coyote showed his disgust with me. "Because powers greater than you or me set it up to be ambiguous. It is not up to us to question the ambiguity of being. It is only up to us to learn the qualities of the soul through the ambiguity of being."

"You mean we're forced to think?" I asked.

"We are forced to think, and we are forced to act. And all our thinking and all our acting have the character of ambiguity, of the mingling of such things as love and larceny."

"The crèche and the cross," I said.

"Absolutely," he said. "The crèche and the cross. You are born and you die. What's in between is love and larceny. Yourself and others. It's for the developement of your soul that you have to puzzle it out. And act."

"And the Grinch?"

"He's above it all. Doesn't want to get involved. He's superior."

"You're a thief in the night, Coyote."

He looked shocked. "What do you mean? My heart is full of love! I would never steal from anyone!"

"You just stole the comfortable superior cynicism of the Unitarian Universalists on Christmas Eve!"

He grinned. "Consider it a Christmas present."

"Thanks," I said, with just a touch of sarcasm.

"The only reason I was out there in the Santa outfit hustling some bucks was so I could buy you a Christmas present."

I had a horrible greedy feeling that I had shortchanged myself by being so righteous.

"I could take you back there," I said.

"It's okay," he said, "I gave you the gift of ambiguity."

"The gift that keeps on giving," I said.

"Right," he said. "You can drop me off at the Salvation Army. I have something I picked up for them."

I checked my socks.

COYOTE THINKS EASTER IS THE MOST NATURAL THING IN THE WORLD

was thinking of going to the salad bar at the health food emporium when the odor of baked goods wafted through my outside study entrance. I knew there was a blessing in the offing. I opened the door and in came Coyote with a plate of hot cross buns.

"Rob a church?" I asked.

"Think of it as a miracle," he said. "You were thinking a good thought and here I am, the symbol of joy, indulgence, and selfishness borne on the sweet wings of spring to rescue you."

"What have you been sniffing, Coyote?"

"The spring, the spring, the glorious spring!" he cried. He did a dippy pirouette. I caught the plate of hot cross buns as it headed for the sofa.

We embraced, and he licked my face. I did not return the lick. He knows I'm uptight about canine licks. We accept our differences. I wiped my face with my handkerchief. The expressions of love you get are not always the ones you fantasize. I would rather have the real than the fantasy most days.

I glanced at my word processor, but he caught my glance and said, "No! No sermon! We're going to celebrate Easter."

"Unitarian Universalists don't celebrate Easter," I said.

"So you don't want any hot cross buns?"

"Well," I said, "I could observe the form without the substance."

"No! We have to have a confession of faith. You have to pay the piper if you're going to dance."

He held up a hot cross bun as if he were teasing a large dog.

"Come on, boy. Confess! Confess!"

I lunged for the bun, all thoughts of the salad bar out of my mind. He kept it just out of my reach by simply levitating.

"Coyote, that is just a hot cross bun; some bread with frosting.

Man does not live by hot cross buns alone. We must be reasonable. We cannot be forced by deities to profess belief in what we don't believe."

Hypocritical sympathy suffused his features. "Oh, pardon me! I forgot you don't believe in magic." He started to get himself and his hot cross buns together as though to leave.

"Coyote, I believe in you!"

"Only when I bribe you with hot cross buns."

"The deities have to produce benefits for humans if they want to be believed in," I said.

He looked sad. "You're right. And you have everything you need, so you don't believe anymore."

"Coyote, let's compromise. Let's discuss the meaning of Easter while we energize the discussion by eating those now merely warm cross buns."

He mused and said, "Like the Walrus and the Carpenter inviting the oysters for a walk while they spoke of cabbages and kings?"

"Exactly."

"Like the lobbyists and members of Congress discussing democracy while eating up the voters?"

"Yes, yes," I said. "Because we know a hot cross bun's joy in being is to provide energy for the spiritually enlightened to dialogue on the meaning of such things as Easter."

He licked my face again, and we lit into the hot cross buns.

"Now," Coyote said, as he licked his paws and I licked my fingers, "I'm going to demonstrate that Easter is the most natural thing in the world."

With that incantation, there was a great rushing noise and the room began to spin. In a moment we were standing on a desert hillside.

"Coyote, I have a feeling this isn't New Mexico."

He shushed me, and we joined a large crowd of ragged and rather desperate-looking people. I was glad I was wearing my Birks because everyone else was in sandals. They were friendly and smiled, and I realized someone was addressing them. Someone said he was an itinerant rabbi.

"You know this man?" I asked Coyote.

"He's one of us," Coyote whispered.

The gist of the rabbi's message was that the rich and powerful and the clever thought they owned the earth and could do whatever they wanted to it. That's not true said the rabbi. The earth really belongs to all people, even the meek and the poor and the people who have been dispossessed by the greed of the rich, powerful, and clever. God made life and the earth for all of us. The crowd, being mostly meek, poor, and dispossessed thought the rabbi ought to run for President. Others questioned whether he really would be able to change things since the rich, the powerful, and the clever had rigged the system so it couldn't be reformed. They had well-paid theorists who wrote articles explaining that God wanted things as they are. The rabbi was saying that wasn't true. God loved everyone.

There was a commotion at the edge of the crowd. Some soldiers came marching through and arrested the rabbi. The Captain of the Guard said the rabbi had to be arrested because he had spoken against God. Everyone should go home. Show up the next day for the execution. Then the Captain of the Guard laughed and said, "If God is on the rabbi's side, maybe God will save him."

Of course God didn't save the rabbi. I was pretty depressed. But Coyote said, "Wait, he's one of us. It's not over 'til it's over!"

The next thing I knew people were running around saying, "The rabbi didn't die after all. God raised him from the dead."

I asked Coyote, "Is it the same rabbi?"

"What difference does it make if it's the same rabbi?" he said. "The point is there is always someone—rabbi, socialist, labor organizer, consumer advocate—who does not buy the idea that the rich and powerful and clever are rich, powerful, and clever because God wants them to be. There are always voices saying that the heart of being human is something other than getting power, wealth, and education."

He grinned, and went on. "It's a coyote world. The gods always have the last laugh. The joke is on those who strive for what the world says is good. It's good to be comfortable and well-fed, but that's not the heart of being human. Understanding and empathy have nothing to do with riches, power, or cleverness. The rabbi is only a manifestation of the truth. There will always be incarnations of the truth, the heart of being human. The chances are, when you meet such an incarnation in a woman or a man, she or he won't be rich or powerful."

Before I could respond, a great dust storm came up. First thing I knew I was standing on a lovely island among a group of islands with a deep blue sea surrounding them. The sky was soft, the air was cool and clean, and the fields and arbors were just greening out.

We saw some folks in a grove, and we headed that way. They were friends of Coyote. There seemed to be a little species confusion, for they were part naked human and part furry animals. There were some apparently all-humans, too, rather voluptuous and naked and quaffing something that looked appealing after the dusty journey. At the edge of the grove, people were massaging each other's feet and backs, and some were unabashedly making love. It was the sort of delinquency that isn't tolerated anymore by right-thinking people.

Coyote seemed to want to shed my company, so I joined a party. The wine was not distinguished, but it went down well. Frankly, the rest of the trip is a bit of a haze. I'm glad there were no tabloid reporters there.

Sometime later I found Coyote swapping raunchy stories with some well-preserved older satyrs. He introduced me as his friend, the reasonable man. They all looked at me with benign pity. One of them said, "Coyote says you don't believe in Easter."

I said, "I thought you were all pagans. I thought you didn't believe in Easter either."

I must have said something very funny, for they all roared with laughter. One of the satyrs whopped Coyote on the back and said, "I thought you were kidding, Coyote. I wouldn't have believed it if I hadn't heard it from him himself."

They all had a great laugh and I felt like a jerk. However, it seemed okay to be a jerk in such a fine company of healthy old satyrs. They offered me a cup of the hair of the dog.

Coyote said, "The pagans started Easter. Easter has always been about the renewal of life. The pagans knew the earth renews itself as a natural thing. Those who understand the earth would have us live as the earth lives. We have our seasons of winter and joyous summer and the in-between. As the seasons come and go, so a person's life comes and goes and changes. Natural and fulfilling. So the crones and old satyrs over there are not anxious. They have had full lives in all its seasons and they rejoice in memories of the pleasures of life."

I raised my cup, which was running over, and we drank to the spring.

Taking Coyote aside, I asked, "What about that other Easter?"

He tossed off his cup of wine and looked at me with a slightly vacant expression as though wishing I was a little less dense.

"One Easter is Easter as humans imagine life could have been. Maybe even once was, when humans lived in harmony with earth. The other Easter is Easter as it has to be in a world where the rich, powerful, and clever proclaim themselves God's favorites; the earth is theirs to consume. In the latter Easter, Easter has to be subversive rather than openly celebrated as it is here."

"So," I recited, "Easter is celebrating life's renewal. In some cultures it can be celebrated openly, and in others it has to be a subversive activity."

"Says something about a culture," he said sadly.

Suddenly we were back in my office and the plate of hot cross buns was empty.

Coyote smiled and said, "You tricked me!"

"How did I trick you, old Trickster?"

"I swore when I came in I was not going to let you get a sermon out of this. I was going to lead you in the paths of decadence for my name's sake."

I hugged him and then, on impulse, I licked his face.

COYOTE WANTS TO KNOW
WHAT'S ALL THIS GOD-TALK?

hadn't seen Coyote around, what with the cold weather, I guess. So I was surprised to see him lounging in the passenger seat when I came out of the church.

"Good heater," he commented. "Okay stereo."

"You want better transportation," I said, "hang out at better churches."

"The elite with better transportation see coyotes only as road hazards," he said. "They don't see the magic."

"Where you been?" I asked.

"Arizona. Chasing roadrunners, dodging Cadillacs," he replied.

"How come you're back?"

"Prayers," he said.

"Prayers?" I didn't figure it.

"Prayers," he said emphatically. "Prayers from members of this very congregation!"

"I didn't know there was any praying going on in this congregation," I said. "I'll have to investigate. See what can be done. Can't have people disturbing our minor deity on vacation."

"You're the cause of it!" he said reproachfully and accusingly.

"Me? What did I do?"

"Talking about God. First it was the Republicans, then it was the three sermons on God, then Christmas. More than some of your people can stand!"

"And they got in touch with *you*? Through prayer?"

"Something had to be done, so they appealed to a higher power."

"Coyote," I said, "this doesn't make sense. Some of the people who apparently don't like to hear the word 'God' in a Unitarian Universalist church are appealing through prayer to a minor deity such as yourself to help them in their time of need?"

"Why doesn't it make sense?" he asked all innocence.

I thought to myself that maybe I've been in this business too long.

I'm missing the subtleties.

"Well," I said, "I may be simpleminded, but I would think people who didn't want God mentioned in the church wouldn't appeal to a god, even a minor one."

"Ah!" he said. "I see your point. Perhaps it is the contrarian in them that liked the irony."

"And what is your position on this?" I asked, really quite puzzled. I mean, I thought the gods liked being mentioned in church.

"It's got to stop, Reverend, it's got to stop."

I started the truck. "I think we need some nourishment and stimulation for this conversation," I said.

"Right!" he said, cheerful now. "Theology goes better on a sugar high!"

"It's a manic pastime," I agreed.

We wheeled into the donut shop and, after a little sniffing with the other coyotes to catch up with what had been happening, we settled down with some sugar bombs and caffeine, the churchperson's drug of choice.

"Explicate this conundrum, please," I said.

"Thou shalt have no gods before me," he said sternly.

"Oh, Coyote, come on! Be serious! That's Yahweh's line. Next thing, you'll be handing me two tablets of stone."

"A few guidelines might not be amiss."

"Where was this place in Arizona?" I asked.

"Top secret!" he smirked.

"But still accessible to humanist prayers?" I muttered under my breath.

"The gods have conferred," he said pompously, "and they forbid you to teach from that book *A History of God*."

"The gods are forbidding me to use a book on theology?" I was incredulous.

"It makes the concept of God too comfortable," he said, "which makes the gods uncomfortable."

"You mean it makes you human creations! Is that it? Is that what's getting to your egos?"

"Of course," he said smugly. "You Unitarian Universalist humanist heretics don't like being called children of God and we gods don't like being called the creations of humans."

"And how do the humanists fit into this? Why did you respond to the non-God faction in this church? What have they ever done for you?"

He looked down his snout as though I was quite naive. "Atheists take their gods seriously!" he said vehemently. "They do not condescend to make gods into human creations, into human *ideas.*" He spat out the last word. "They deny that gods exist, which means they take the existence of gods seriously. Actually the gods love atheists. Atheists deny the existence of gods, but the gods don't deny the existence of atheists. Which is why atheists exist. Everything exists at the pleasure of the gods. You see the irony of it, don't you?"

He smirked, held out a donut, examined it smilingly, and popped it into non-existence. I could see him doing the same to an atheist who had at last bored him. Perhaps we are all sugar-coated donuts waiting in a box for the pleasure of a god. Not a pleasant thought while in conversation with one.

"I see what you mean," I said. "You think my recent god-talks do not take the gods seriously enough as existing quite apart from human imagining."

"Or not existing," he said. "Your free choice."

"But you don't like us to call you human creations, is that it? Is that where the guidelines are necessary?"

"Exactly!" he said. "Now if you will pay the waitress and excuse me, I'll be getting back to the Superstition Mountains of Arizona."

"Not so fast, fur face!" I said.

He looked aghast.

I had his attention.

I put my finger in front of his schnoz and wagged it. "Let me tell you something, fur face," I said. "You gods have been playing hide-and-seek with humans for hundreds of centuries. You have been playing with our minds, driving people crazy with your now-you-see-us, now-you-don't. You have been creating wars. You have been deceiving beautiful young maidens, and maybe as far as I know some sweet young boys, too. You hide in the storm and refuse to let the electron microscopes or the telescopes see you. Yet you tantalize the creationists. You endorse the supposed divine right of kings and the burning of books and maybe even the burning of a few Unitarians and Universalists who were trying to appeal to your better nature and hide your demonic side. You have a lot of gall to demand any sort of respect from humans or belief in you. We could have done a lot better without you."

"Yeah?" he sneered. "Look how you screwed up Eden."

"We didn't screw up! It was your stupid rule that we shouldn't eat the apples! You should have known better than to put a man and a woman in an orchard and not expect them to eat the apples."

"That was Yahweh's idea," he said defensively. "I didn't have anything to do with that."

"Sorry, fur face, you've got to do better than that! If you exist, really and objectively, then you'd better write a few guidelines for yourselves down there at that resort in the Superstition Mountains!"

He looked at me as a parent might look at a child showing its first symptoms of adolescent rebellion. A mix of "who the hell does he think he is?" and a cautious sense of pride. For my part, I was feeling definite warnings of going too far. But they were swept away with feelings of indignation.

I leaned forward in his face. "Let's just take Eden. And don't blame it on Yahweh. Every one of you is cut from the same cloth! You're all a bunch of tricksters, from Job's god to the Pope's. Take Eden! You created a man and a woman in an ideal environment. You could have set it up so they were protected and lived the life of bliss all humans hunger for and never achieve for more than a weekend. Or you could have provided an operating manual for life. Don't have too many children, don't pollute the air because you have to breathe it. Some simple rules, which if followed would make for cooperative and humane interactions between humans, for which they would praise the gods for having made such a wondrous creation. But no, you had to introduce pain and sickness and old age and death and children being victims and greed and treachery and existential meaninglessness. Look at this beautiful scenery. Why couldn't you just as easily have created a beautiful interactive loving human social order?"

"Well," he said, "if it isn't the Reverend Dr. Job!"

"Job was right and you know it, old Trickster. Job is one of the oldest stories of humanity, and it just proves that humanity has been on to the injustice of the gods for several thousand years."

"Would you have really preferred the life of the Garden of Eden? One boring day after another in paradise? Sort of like retirement in Santa Fe?"

It was time for the adolescent to be uncomfortable. "No," I had to admit, "it has been an adventure trying to figure it out."

"Actually," he said, "we did try a creation with complete instructions for happiness, and it was a total failure. The creatures laid around complaining that they were victims and didn't have any say in how they ran their lives. It was a socialist paradise, and the ungrateful wretches voted Republican. So we scratched that and started over."

I had another donut to sustain the manic sugar high and said, "I know it's unwise to question the word of a god, but I think you're making that up."

"We make everything up," he said.

"So you're responsible!" I accused.

"Oh, no," he said, "it all works itself out however it works itself out."

"You can't have it both ways!" I said with the firm conviction of an adolescent speaking to a parent.

"But it is both ways!" he said. "It's light and dark. It's good and bad. It's mean and it's grand. It's petty and it's glorious."

I began to doubt my certainty. I was dealing with the Trickster, all right. "Coyote," I asked, "Why can't life be simple and good?"

He looked at me with a certain kindly tolerant look that was both comforting and maddening: the parental "gotcha!"

"Life wouldn't be life if it were only simple and good," he explained. "You are given life by the gods. Or chance, if you prefer. Whichever, you are given life. It is yours to make good or evil. It is not up to us to make it good or evil for you."

"I'd do it differently were I a god," I said.

"Of course you would," he said soothingly, "but thank god you're not a god. You've got all you can handle being a person."

"It seems like more than I can handle sometimes."

"Let me explicate the conundrum for you," he said. "You know, you humans, at least the intellectual elite among the humans, think the cutting edge in human discovery is discovering the limits of the universe, the origins, the design, the micro-structure. That's not the cutting edge of life. That's just the intellectual cutting edge. The universe is working itself out. But life, within the framework of the universe, is life discovering what life is, what life means, what life could be. To have a rule book would be a denial of what life is about."

"I still think a rule book would have been helpful. Or at least some hints!"

"You have hints in the myths and religious stories. You created them out of the collective human experience. Get in touch with life as it has left its record in the air."

"So you're agreeing that we create the gods?"

"No, you are creating stories about what is meaningful for a human life, what is good conduct and what is painful and evil."

I asked, "What did the gods create when the gods created life?"

"Something that was missing in the chaos and order of the lifeless time and space," he said. "Creation that could meditate upon itself and create itself. Create heaven and hell. For itself and for others. Creation able to choose how it would go. Free will, ol' buddy!"

He appeared ready to leave. I had the feeling the interview was at an end.

"Give me a clue, your grace," I said, smiling. "I need to take home something for the money I've spent on coffee and donuts!"

"Life is a paisley," he said.

"A paisley?" I repeated, thinking my hearing aid had closed down.

"A moving paisley," he corrected himself. "A flowing paisley. At any given moment you can stop the paisley design and print it on your necktie, but that's just a snapshot showing life's color and richness and complex design in one instant. Life itself is a liquid paisley design. You're beginning to understand it in chaos theory and social theory. Life is open, and the Trickster is everywhere."

I grinned. "I'm holding out for Eden and an operating manual. I think the gods are copping out. They just don't know what they're doing."

He shook his head, wondering what it would take to get enlightenment into this child of God. "I will spell it out for you," he said. "You are right; we gods have copped out. We gave you freedom. Now the question is whether you cop out. Because you are now the gods in charge of your own creation. You are life discovering what life is and, whether you like it or not, creating what life will become. Think self-conscious, self-creating, flowing paisley, inventing ever-changing patterns and richness. The gift the gods gave you is to participate in that."

And with that he vanished, leaving me with a littered table and the bill. Well, haven't you ever been left by a god with the cleanup and the bill? All you can do is smile, pay up, and leave a clean table for the next customer.

COYOTE IS CONFUSED ABOUT POWER

 was sitting at the breakfast table with a cup of coffee and *The New Mexican* trying once again to understand Bosnia. As a concerned liberal, I know I should have a position. I find my pacifism and my humanitarianism in conflict.

I heard the sliding door from the patio open and looked around to see: Coyote? A strange coyote; I wasn't sure it was really himself. He was dressed in combat fatigues, spit-shined paratrooper boots, and sunglasses.

"Jesus, Coyote, is that *you?*" I cried.

Grim, he swaggered over to the table and sat down straddling a dining chair backwards. "Get me some coffee!" he ordered.

"Coyote!" I protested. "You just don't come into a person's house and *demand* a cup of coffee! What's gotten into you?"

"We're tired of being pushed around! We're tired of you humans not believing in us! We're tried of being cynically used to promote Santa Fe style. I'm telling you, bubba," he said, "We're taking over and it's a new day!"

"So," I said, "take over. Then what?"

"I dunno," he said. "That's what I wanted to talk to you about."

"Coyote," I said, "what's happened?"

He was silent. Then he took off his sunglasses. There were tears in his eyes. "My cousin got wiped out on I-25 night before last. Tried to make it across, but misjudged the speed of the truck and the width of the roadway. You know we can't go *anywhere* without having to cross one of your damned roads! So we're going to take over. Tear up the interstates! You want to live in Santa Fe, then *stay* in Santa Fe. Don't go tearing off someplace else endangering peace-loving coyotes innocently chasing roadrunners."

Becoming ministerial, I got up and poured him a cup of coffee and cut some fresh bread. I opened up some marmalade. He softened, spread the marmalade lavishly, ate it, and then held out the empty plate wordlessly. I humored him. Being obeyed seemed to bring him back to himself. He ate the second slice slowly and sipped his coffee.

"What is it about power," he asked, "that makes folks so mean? Give people a gun and they think they have to use it. Give them a car and they think they have to blast down the road leaving dead coyotes in their exhaust."

"Give them a legislature," I said, "and they think they can take from the poor and give to the rich."

He gave the power salute. "*Eat* the rich!" he shouted.

"Easy for you to say!" I said. "For me it would be cannibalism."

He looked nonplussed. "That doesn't upset you when I say, 'Eat the rich!'?"

"It's an interesting idea, but it's not going to happen."

"Come the revolution, when the gods and the animals get together, we'll eat the rich!" He glared at me. "What's your net worth?"

"I don't qualify as a square meal, Coyote."

"Let's see your tax return," he said.

"You show me yours," I said.

"I just dematerialize when the IRS comes round," he said and laughed. "Drives 'em nuts!"

"So," he went on, "why *not* eat the rich? They deserve it."

"That's why they're rich," I said, "so they won't be just desserts."

"I'm being serious and you make jokes!"

"Your seriousness is a joke to the rich and powerful," I said. "They will either buy you or kill you. That is how they keep from being eaten. It's called power."

"Why can't they share?" he asked, with a little hint of a whine.

"Because they think that if they shared, they wouldn't be rich very long. They'd be poor. And the way things are going on the planet, the poor may be eaten."

"So is that the reason for power: to keep from being eaten?" he asked.

"No," I said, "that is the rationalization for power. Rich people like to tell themselves they are simply being sensible in a dog-eat-dog world, looking out for their own interests. Powerful people, many of whom are not rich in dollars, tell themselves they are being realistic and are just looking out for the general welfare, keeping the lid on human savagery."

"Then the rich and the powerful are not the same?"

"Sometimes they are, but often they are not. Often the rich don't know the power game. Often the power players don't care about being particularly rich. But the rich and the powerful have a lot in common. They tend to take care of each other. And they agree in despising those who are neither rich nor powerful."

He reflected for a moment, then asked, "Did I hear you say the rich and powerful are fooling themselves that what they are doing is reasonable and realistic? Is that what you said?"

"Yes, that's what I said."

"What do you think they are really doing?"

"They are addicts, Coyote."

"They aren't either!" he said indignantly. "Everyone knows addicts live in the inner city and commit crimes and have to be locked up."

"They are *addicts*, Coyote! The rich can never be rich enough to feel safe. The powerful can never have enough control over people to feel safe. They find it very hard to let go and relax and just live. They are not satisfied being comfortable. They are not satisfied by give-and-take. They don't know why. They just know they have to stay rich and stay powerful or—well, they can't bear to think of the alternative."

"You mean they think they'd be eaten?" he asked.

"Worse than that, Coyote. They might become nobody. That's the fear they're running away from and trying to satisfy addictively. Power over others means they feel real. Power is their drug of choice."

"So what's healthy in your opinion? Being poor and powerless? Being meek and inheriting the earth?"

"No, although I can see you might have thought so, given the history of Christian theology in which the meek are falsely assured they will inherit the earth."

"You think the meek get eaten?"

"It usually works that way, Coyote. But that's not the only choice, being meek and being eaten or being rich or powerful and surviving. Because you see, they are both afraid of being eaten. The rich and powerful know they can always lose it through a market disaster or a revolution. If that happens, they're going to have to take some fast meek lessons, because everyone loves a fallen mighty. How they love to beat up on the once haughty!"

"You humans are nastier than I realized," he said reflectively.

"Some are, some aren't," I said. "Humans have been taught by the mighty that might makes right. The mighty are righteous by definition because the mighty do the defining of what is righteous. There is a tricky little reversal in Christianity that makes Christianity popular among the meek. It tells them that in the afterlife things are going to be reversed and the meek will get theirs."

"And the rich and powerful will get theirs?"

"They will get eternally gnawed on by voracious insatiable devils in hell," I said.

"Why didn't the rich and powerful stamp out Christianity?"

"Because the rich and powerful see that Christianity makes the poor and the meek content to wait for the afterlife to even the score. Which is fine with the rich and powerful who are interested in getting their addiction sated in this life. Besides, they figure they can buy salvation by giving a large gift to the church. They figure even God can be bought, which shows how irrational their addiction is."

"You said rich and powerful and meek and poor are not the only possibilities. Please set my spirit at rest, because I don't like being poor and meek, and I hear you saying that riches and power are an addict's game. Nevertheless, I tend to think the addicts have the best of it. I suppose you have a golden mean of some sort, my dear philosopher?"

"I know how you love sarcasm," I said, "but you're putting me on the defensive."

"Well, get off it!" he shouted. "Give us some hope!"

Which was just what I needed. I shouted right back, "Who the hell do you think you are, coming in here, interrupting my breakfast like you own the place?"

He looked at me calmly and said, "I am your God, that's who I am."

"Well, it doesn't give you the right to come barging into my life and ordering me around!" I was getting indignant.

He was shocked. "Of course I have the right to come barging into your life and ordering you around. That's what gods do! What's the point of being a god if I can't bully you?"

"Look, buster," I said. "All I have to do is stop believing in you, and you're out that door without a donut to your name."

He looked at me, incredulous at first. And then the light came into his eyes. "You mean we need each other?" he asked quietly.

"Yes," I said.

We were silent, just looking at each other with a mixture of respect and humor and love and frustration. I filled our coffee cups.

"Coyote," I said, "the old way has to go. The old gods of royal power have to go; they don't work anymore. Humans who can't give them up will die, and evolution will proceed and the old gods and their worshippers will be history. The old human relations based on the old gods have to go. The power of the gun. The power of keeping people ignorant. The political secrets. The elite. The rich. They all have to go if the next stage in evolution is going to happen. They are probably not going to go peacefully and willingly because they are addicted to the old ways of being a somebody. There are new ways of being a somebody. Needing each other. Sharing what we know and finding the synergism of that. There is great power in that. There seems to be the power of what the future wants to be. The new ways may or may not happen. Can't predict! No one would have predicted five hundred years ago that we'd have evolved this far."

He finished my thought for me. "Evolved into being aware we need each other? Is that it? Is that the difference?"

"Yes," I said. "That's the revolutionary idea. We've always needed each other. It's the synergy of being human. It's just the awareness that's new. It's been growing. Democracy is its theory. Sharing information instantaneously is its present way of coming into being."

"Give me some examples," he said.

"Bosnia—we see the tragedy of the old power ways. The old power ways, even when dressed up with the latest technology, are powerless to resolve it. Israel—we see the tragedy of the old religious ways. No love or forgiveness or compassion there. No sense of needing each other. So it is never resolved. Health care—a compassionate idea based on the idea that we need each other; undermined and delayed and fought by powerful leaders who can feel only their need to satisfy their addiction to power and money. Population control. The information about what overpopulation is doing is expanding. We hope the message will expand faster than the population. The measure that it is happening is that old members of Congress are deciding to retire; money and power aren't as much fun as they used to be. The old rich and the old powerful get no respect from those who know where the evolutionary action is."

He stood up and gave a mock salute. "So," he said, "you don't need a weatherperson to know which way the wind is blowing?"

"There's no predicting the weather, Coyote. But I'll bet on it being stormy before it gets calm and fair."

I got up and gave him a hug and whispered in his ear, "Just remember, we need each other."

"So what are we coyotes supposed to do while you humans are working out your addictions?"

"We need new gods on which to model our conduct," I said. "You must model irreverence and intelligence and ingenious solutions."

"That's me!" he said. "Master of ingenious solutions."

"And always optimistic even when they don't work," I added.

"Speak for yourself," he said.

"I am," I said.

"So, describe more fully this new conduct you want us divinities to model for you?"

"Intelligence. Generosity. Compassion. Cooperativeness. Openness to new ideas. Mindfulness—being here now. Letting go of control. Self-discipline for the common good. Honoring what is to be; that the roots of what is to be are here and now."

"Will that make me rich?" he asked.

"You'll survive, and your pups will survive," I said.

"Will it make me powerful?" he asked.

"It'll make you happy," I said.

"Will you still respect me?" he asked shyly.

"I'll bake you fresh bread every Saturday and buy you gourmet marmalade," I said.

"I'll take it!" he said.

And with that, he took off the camouflage fatigues and the paratrooper boots and rolled them up and put them in the trash compactor.

"I'll keep the shades," he said. "They're cool."

"Always be cool," I said, and he vanished, leaving only a friendly grin in the air. If you look real hard, you can see his friendly grin, too. It's a message from the cosmos we should keep on trying.

DOÑA COYOTE IS THINKING ABOUT ENTERING THE UNITARIAN UNIVERSALIST MINISTRY

 oyote and I had made fools of ourselves at the Unitarian Universalist General Assembly. Doña Coyote and Nancy pretended they didn't know us and went off to one of the 530 meetings with notebooks in hand.

I was feeling pretty good as we ate breakfast, but Coyote was downcast. I thought maybe it was that all the cheerful atheists and skeptics were wearing on him. Finally he looked at me seriously and said, "It's all your fault!"

"What's my fault?" I asked airily.

"Breaking up my happy home."

"Coyote, I didn't know. How could I break up your happy home? What do you mean?"

He stuck his snout in the air. "It wouldn't have happened if you hadn't invited us to this General Assembly."

"What is the problem, my dear *compadre*?"

He sighed a great world-is-coming-to-an-end sigh and said, "Doña Coyote has been turned on by the Unitarian Universalists. She thinks the feminist ecological theology is right on. She says she misjudged the UUs. Now she sees you people as the last great hope for saving the planet."

"Wow!" I said. "A conversion! Considering the things she's said about me, that's quite an event. I would think you'd be delighted."

"I am not delighted," he hissed. Then he yelled so everyone in the convention foyer could hear him. "I am not delighted!" Coyote glared at them all, but no one paid him any attention. He looked at me and whimpered, "I am not delighted!"

"Okay, okay, so you're not delighted. What are you not delighted about?"

"It's those damn women," he hissed.

"Careful, Coyote. Let's be politically correct. What have the women done to us now?"

"They're taking over!" he said, indignant.

"That will be news to a lot of women," I said. "What are they taking over?"

"They are taking over the Unitarian Universalist denomination. If the UUs are the last great hope for the planet, that means the future of the planet will be in the hands of women."

I wasn't sure how to deal with such a heretical tone, so I stirred my coffee vigorously.

"Stop stirring your coffee!" he said. "You don't stir black coffee."

"I'll stir any damn thing I want to stir," I retorted.

I said it with annoyance and wondered at my own anxiety. Maybe I needed an attitude adjustment myself. Bits of nostalgia for male chauvinism might be lingering in my consciousness, lowering it.

"What makes you think UU women are taking over?" I asked.

"Doña Coyote said to me, 'Coyote, did you notice that all the mid-level power positions here are filled by strong women? Did you notice how in charge the women clergy feel? Did you feel, Coyote, that the UU women are not trying to make it in a man's game anymore, but act as though they had already made it in their own game? Have you noticed, Coyote, that all the great men ministers are has-beens like your friend what's-his-name?'"

I put my coffee mug down with a crash. "She said what?"

"I'm sorry, but that's what she said."

"Doña Coyote thinks I'm a has-been and can't even remember my name?"

"Sorry," he said, but he was grinning.

"God, Coyote, what am I going to do? A has-been? Old what's-his-name?"

Coyote put a fraternal paw on my shoulder and hugged me. "Relax," he said, "just ride in the back of the bus and let these young women figure out where we're going."

I thought about it. "Coyote, I am their leader! Which way did they go?"

"Relax," he said soothingly. "You now are, in Jungian terms, a senex, a male crone."

"Oh, shut up, Coyote! I am not a—senex!"

He was tremendously pleased. "Good! I've got you in a foul mood, and that greatly relieves my foul mood." He was one great smile from ear to ear.

"I think I'd rather hang out with Jesus," I said.

"I am much more understanding," he said. "Jesus is too good for you. You and I are men of the world, rich in dark experience, deeply imbued with soul, content to make do with the possible and enjoy it."

I was flattered. "Hey, you're right, Coyote."

"We hang out on the Zen sunny side of the Plaza and observe and whittle and leave the power trips to women."

"What are the young men going to be doing," I asked, worried about my male offspring.

"They will have to adjust," he said. "Perhaps they will find meaning in raising children, keeping house, and doing volunteer work. Good Republican family values."

"One thing about being a trickster," I said, "is there's always irony to enjoy."

Coyote turned somber. "I haven't told you the whole thing."

"What is it, Coyote? Tell me, brother."

He sighed a very deep sigh. "This time the irony has gone too far. This time the trick is not funny."

"Tell me, Coyote. I will understand and comfort you as a well-bonded male brother should. We will hug and cry and be present for each other. Tell me. You'll see. It'll be okay."

"Doña Coyote told me at breakfast that she is thinking of entering the Unitarian Universalist ministry."

I fell off my stool laughing.

He looked at me on the floor helplessly doubled up laughing. "Thanks for all the male-bonding and support!" he snarled.

I got up and wiped my eyes and clambered back on the stool. "Coyote, they'll never accept her in the ministry. She's a coyote."

"Shows how out of touch you are," he snorted. "Antiquated senex!" he shouted. "She's already got a hundred signatures on a petition to combat species-ism in ministerial entrance requirements. It promises to become an issue in the next presidential election whether the UU ministry should be restricted to humans."

I stared. "Coyote, they can't do that!"

"It's the way things are going," he said.

"Coyote, does this mean we're going to have horned toads and squirrels coming to church on Sunday?"

"I suppose so," he said. "It's going to take some welcoming action on your part to make them feel welcome. They're used to being shooed out of the churches they've entered."

"Am I expected to sermonize to the birds?"

"St. Francis did," he said mildly.

"I'm not ready for this, Coyote."

"Neither am I. But you have to admit, it has possibilities for diversity. Think how species-chauvinist churches have been. Think how differently people would feel about hamburgers if some of their fellow parishioners were cows. How would people feel about eating chicken if some members were perched on the back of the pews?"

"Coyote, this is nuts!"

"Is it?" he asked.

"No," I said, "it isn't. It's just such a radical idea I didn't want to accept it. But it's probably no more radical than the idea that women should be ordained seemed to men 200 years ago."

"Exactly," he said. "Progress."

"Coyote, if you really feel that way, how come you're upset over Doña Coyote considering the ministry? It sounds as though you're basically in agreement with her."

"You're right," he said. "I am in agreement with her. I do think all species have to be united in spirit if the planet is to survive. Either that or eliminate the humans. It's just that . . . " He stopped.

"It's just what?" I asked tenderly.

"It's just . . . " He wiped his eyes with his paws and then turned toward me with a distraught expression. "It's just—Oh, damn!"

I held his paws. He took a deep breath and said, "It's just that I don't know if I can stand being the spouse of a graduate student."

"Now, Coyote, it will only be four years and then," I said cheerily, "you'll be the spouse of a minister!"

He looked at me with virtual hatred. "A big damn help you are in cheering me up and saving my marriage."

He pouted. We sat there in comradely confusion.

"Why did I ever let you write that damn book?" he said. "Why did I ever let you talk us into coming to General Assembly? It has ruined my life!"

I felt terrible. I had ruined my friend's life. I also had to face my own senexery, and I wasn't feeling gracious about that.

I felt a gentle paw on my shoulder, as did Coyote. We both turned to see Doña Coyote looking radiant.

"How are you boys this morning?" she asked with a grin.

We exchanged glum glances, then put on happy faces, and answered in chorus: "Fine! Fine! Couldn't be better."

"Wonderful!" she said.

Then looking lovingly at Coyote, she said, "Coyote, my dear, I have made my decision."

"And what is that?" he asked with feigned enthusiasm.

"I am going to run for the Senate!" she announced.

We looked at her, stunned. Then we cheered. Doña patted Coyote's muzzle and said, "Will you be my campaign manager, dear?"

Coyote grinned. "Can we do dirty tricks?"

"Of course," she said. "Why do you think I asked you?"

So this morning in the foyer of the church next to the coffee, you will find petitions to make it legal for coyotes to run for the Senate.